LETTERS OF
SIR JOSHUA REYNOLDS

T0382044

SIR JOSHUA REYNOLDS

The portrait painted for the Royal Gallery
in Florence. *From Townley's engraving, 1777*

LETTERS OF
SIR JOSHUA REYNOLDS

Collected and Edited

by

FREDERICK WHILEY HILLES, Ph.D.

Instructor in English at Yale University

CAMBRIDGE

AT THE UNIVERSITY PRESS

1929

CAMBRIDGE
UNIVERSITY PRESS

University Printing House, Cambridge CB2 8BS, United Kingdom

Cambridge University Press is part of the University of Cambridge.

It furthers the University's mission by disseminating knowledge in the pursuit of
education, learning and research at the highest international levels of excellence.

www.cambridgc.org
Information on this title: www.cambridge.org/9781107495036

© Cambridge University Press 1929

First published 1929
First paperback edition 2015

A catalogue record for this publication is available from the British Library

ISBN 978-1-107-49503-6 Paperback

To

C. D. H. & D. W. H.

CONTENTS

ILLUSTRATIONS

PREFACE

Shortly after Sir Joshua's death, an anonymous contributor to the *Gentleman's Magazine*[1] suggested that "by means of the letters which he wrote..., whose merit, no doubt, hath induced those, by whom they were received, to preserve them", a fitting "Life of this eminent painter" might be given to the public. The suggestion met with little or no support. Indeed, it was not until fifty years later that a biographer seriously attempted to collect his correspondence; since when more than twice as many letters have come to light. The increasing interest shown in Dr Johnson by scholars and collectors alike, would seem to justify a collection of the letters of Reynolds, who, it must be remembered, was not only "father of English painting" but founder of the Literary Club and Johnson's *dulce decus*.

To many this collection will seem surprisingly small, since it is to be expected that the letters of a man who rose to such eminence would have been carefully preserved. But like Goldsmith, who "never wrote a letter in his life",[2] Sir Joshua wrote sparingly. He used to say that his friend Astley, the painter, would rather run three miles to deliver his message by word of mouth than venture

1 lxii, ii, 1200.
2 *Letters of Samuel Johnson*, ed. Hill, Oxford, 1892, i, p. v.

to write a note; the same remark applied to himself. "Familiar letters by Sir Joshua", wrote his
pupil, James Northcote, "are...very scarce: he
was too busy and too wise to spend his time in an
occupation which is more congenial to the idle and
the vain, who are commonly very voluminous in
their production of this article".[1] From the same
source we learn that in early life he "was too much
occupied in his studies to dedicate much time to
epistolary correspondence",[2] and in his closing
years, when threatened with blindness, he naturally refrained as much as possible from writing.[3]
Throughout his correspondence we note phrases
which admirably illustrate this. "I write with
continual interruption, having so little to say, and
so little time to say that little, that I believe I should
not have ventured to have wrote, if I had not had

[1] Northcote, i, p. iv.   [2] *Id.* i, 34.
[3] His customary attitude is best brought out in a letter written
July 14, 1786, by his niece, Mary Palmer, to her cousin, William
Johnson, who was in India. "I am affraid my Uncle will as
usual delay writing, tho I know he fully intended it, till it is too
late; however, I have only to assure you that his neglect is not
meant as a slight & that he serves every body the same, always
resolving to write, but never doing it. I am very certain he will
do so now &, when it is too late, will come to me & say, 'Oh,
do give my Love to Mr. Johnson; tell him I meant to write but
am really so much engaged with business that I have not time;
thank him most kindly for the *China* & for the Snuff which he
mentiond in his last letter & tell him I will certainly write by
the next Ship'. Now this, my dear Cousin, will be just what he
will say & perhaps a great deal more; if he does write, so much
the better, but it will be quite an effort if he does."

an opportunity of inclosing my letter in a cover to
Mr. Frazer".[1] "I intended writing to you from
London, and have still a frank for that purpose;
but you know what a bad correspondent I am."[2]
"I am forced to write in a great hurry, and have
little time for polishing my style."[3]

Such passages as these serve to explain the careless and hasty manner in which many of the letters
are written, a manner that is in marked contrast to
that of his published writings. Marks of punctuation
are sparingly used, as might be expected in in-
formal correspondence, but that the author of the
Discourses should be guilty of glaring inaccuracies
in construction and spelling may surprise some
readers. In his letter to Bishop Lowth, for
example, he uses the word *parallelism* three times,
writing it *Parellelisms, parelelisms, paralelism*,[4] and
he frequently mis-spells the names of his most
intimate friends (*e.g. Burk, Keppell, Whitford,
Wilks*).[5] Indeed, so careless is he in such matters
that John Williams, when publishing the letters to
Miss Weston, stated that they would "totally remove the long received idea, that he was the
author of the Discourses delivered at the *Royal
Academy*, or a man of that learning which it has
been generally supposed".[6] To refute this, it is only

1 *V. post*, Letter LVII.   2 *V. post*, Letter LXXI.
3 *V. post*, Letter XII. 4 *V. post*, Letter XLVI.   5 *V. post*, p. 52, n. 5.
6 Pasquin's *Authentic History of the Professors in Painting*, etc.,
London (1796), 60.

necessary to compare his letters with those of the two contemporaries most conspicuous in literature, Goldsmith and Johnson.[1] If the author of *The Vicar of Wakefield* can be guilty of such grammatical mistakes, if the first great English lexicographer can show such inconsistencies in spelling, it is absurd to consider Reynolds illiterate. "Orthography and punctuation, it should be remembered, were laxly regarded in those days, even by men of culture."[2] Not only did he write carelessly, but with great difficulty. Surely Sir Robert Edgcumbe is mistaken in stating that "he had a ready pen, and wrote with but few corrections".[3] I have seen and studied with care the MS. of the lengthy *Apologia* written after his quarrel with the Academy,[4] the original of the character-sketch of Dr Johnson,[5] and many loose folios which were apparently fragments of his *Discourses*, and in every case the pages are covered with additions and corrections. His method of composition was the reverse of Gibbon's;[6] the polish seen in his published writings was the

1 *Letters of Oliver Goldsmith*, ed. Balderston, Cambridge, 1928, 5 *et seq*. *Letters of Samuel Johnson*, i, p. xiv.
2 Leslie and Taylor, ii, 558.
3 Graves and Cronin, 1685. C*f*. Leslie and Taylor, ii, 454.
4 Now in the possession of the Royal Academy. Published by Leslie and Taylor, ii, 558 *et seq*.
5 Now in the possession of Gabriel Wells, Esq., of New York. Published by Leslie and Taylor, ii, 454 *et seq*.
6 *Memoirs of...Gibbon*, ed. Hill, London, 1900, 201.

result of constant revision. Even when composing mere letters, he seems to have made it his practice to write first a rough draft, which he later copied. "I have no doubt", he wrote to Dr Parr, "but that you are surprised to receive a letter in this form. The truth is, this was intended only as a rough draft, but the weakness of my eyes must prove my excuse in not writing it over fair".[1]

It was Boswell's hero Paoli who once declared that he could decide on the character and disposition of a man whose letter he had seen. Certainly the character and disposition of the "dear Knight of Plympton" stand revealed in the letters which follow. No one can say of him what Cowper did of Pope, "the most disagreeable maker of epistles I ever met with" because he "seems to have thought that unless a sentence was well-turned, and every period pointed with some conceit, it was not worth the carriage".[2] For in Sir Joshua's letters the conscious element is lacking, and what is thus lost in correctness and elegance is gained in sincerity. His letters ring true. They are not witty ("I never was a wit in my life");[3] they are not spiced with scandalous anecdotes; but they do reveal that mildness, that genuineness,

1 *V. post*, Letter CLVIII. *Cf. post*, pp. 25, n. 1, 48, n. 1, 103, n. 2, 127, n. 2, 194, n. 2, 196, n. 1, 228, n. 1.
2 *Works of...Pope*, ed. Elwin and Courthope, London, v, 1889, 296.
3 Northcote, i, 123.

that devotion to his calling, for which he was praised by all who knew him.

When Johnson by strength overpowers our mind,
When Montague dazzles, and Burke strikes us blind,
To Reynolds well pleased for relief we must run,
Rejoice in his shadow and shrink from the sun.[1]

Originally a dissertation for the Degree of Doctor of Philosophy in Yale University, this collection consists of one hundred and sixty-one letters, forty-two of which, to the best of my knowledge, have never before been published. Seventy others, obtained from catalogues of autograph collections or from biographies of Sir Joshua's contemporaries, are now for the first time included in a work which deals primarily with Reynolds. Eleven of the remaining forty-nine letters are here published from the originals or photographs of the originals. Where I have not seen the original (or photograph), unless otherwise indicated the text is from the earliest printed version. Those letters that I have seen I have endeavoured to reproduce in the form in which they were written, retaining spelling, capitalization, and what slight punctuation there is. For the sake of ready reference, however, I have placed the date of each letter in the upper right-hand corner, and those dates which in the original appear at the end of the letter are marked with an asterisk. If inaccuracies have crept in, I can only

1 Verses by Mrs Thrale, printed by Leslie and Taylor, ii, 49.

say that every effort has been made to avoid them. Like Boswell, "I have sometimes been obliged to run half over London, in order to fix a date correctly; which, when I had accomplished, I well knew would obtain me no praise, though a failure would have been to my discredit. And after all, perhaps, hard as it may be, I shall not be surprized if omissions or mistakes be pointed out with invidious severity".[1]

"Whatever the success may prove", as Pope has phrased it, "I shall never repent of an undertaking in which I have experienced the candour and friendship of so many persons of merit".[2] The various dealers and private collectors with whom I have come in contact have been more than generous; to each of them I have acknowledged my debt of gratitude in a footnote. Sir Robert Edgcumbe, collateral descendant of Sir Joshua, has throughout given me much aid and encouragement, while Mr W. T. Whitley, Gainsborough's biographer, and such eminent Johnsonians as Mr R. W. Chapman, Mr S. C. Roberts, Dr D. Nichol Smith, and Dr Paget Toynbee, have put me on the track of letters which might otherwise have been overlooked. To my friends Frederick A. Pottle, Arthur E. Case, Miriam R. Small, and Katharine C. Balderston I am indebted for helpful suggestions and criticisms. Mr W. R. M. Lamb, secretary to

1 Boswell's *Life*, i, 1.
2 *Works of...Pope*, Cambridge ed. 261.

the Royal Academy, and Mr Ernest Wright, Librarian, have made my study in the Academy a pleasure, and the staffs of the British Museum and the Yale University Library have considerably lessened the task of editing by their friendly cooperation. Particularly I wish to thank Professor Tinker, whose inspiring lectures aroused in me my first interest in that "large and luminous constellation of British stars" which surrounded Dr Johnson. His scholarly edition of Boswell's letters suggested to me my present undertaking, and his wise counsel and sympathetic understanding have encouraged me to proceed in a work from which I have derived great pleasure during the past four years.

F. W. H.

NEW HAVEN
CONNECTICUT
Sept. 1929

CURRICULUM VITAE

SIR JOSHUA REYNOLDS, 1723–1792

1723, July 16.	Born, at Plympton, Devon.
1740–1742.	In London, apprenticed to Thomas Hudson, portrait painter.
1749–1752.	In Italy, studying.
1753.	Establishes reputation by his portrait of Keppel.
1759.	Writes three essays on painting for Samuel Johnson (published in *The Idler*).
Dec. 26.	Elected a Governor and Guardian of the Foundling Hospital.
1760, July 3.	Buys house in Leicester Fields.
1764, Feb.	Founds (with Johnson) the Club.
1766, May.	Elected to the Society of Dilettanti.
1768, Dec. 14.	Elected President of newly instituted Royal Academy.
1769, April 21.	Knighted.
1772, Sept.	Elected an Alderman of Plympton.
1773, July 9.	Receives D.C.L. from Oxford.
Sept.	Elected Mayor of Plympton.
1774, April–May.	Exhibits his "Three Ladies Adorning a Term of Hymen".
1775, April–May.	Exhibits his "Mrs. Sheridan as Saint Cecilia".
	Elected Member of Academy at Florence.
1778.	Collects and publishes his first seven *Discourses*.
1779, April–May.	Exhibits his "Nativity".
1781, July–Sept.	Travels in Flanders and Holland with Metcalfe.
1782, Feb.	Elected a Steward of the Foundling Hospital.

1784, April–May.   Exhibits his "Mrs. Siddons as the Tragic Muse".

Sept. 1.   Succeeds Ramsay as principal painter to George III.

1785, July–Aug.   Makes second trip to Flanders.

1788, April–May.   Exhibits his "Infant Hercules".

1789, July 13.   Forced to stop painting because of failing eyesight.

1790, Feb. 11.   Resigns as President of Royal Academy after quarrel.

March 15.   Withdraws resignation.

1792, Feb. 23.   Dies.

March 3.   Buried in St Paul's.

BIBLIOGRAPHY[1]

The following are the editions of the works to which I most frequently refer:

Works—*The Works of Sir Joshua Reynolds...in three volumes. To which is prefixed an Account of the Life and Writings of the Author, by Edmond Malone...the second edition corrected.* London, 1798.

Northcote—*The Life of Sir Joshua Reynolds...by James Northcote...the second edition, revised and augmented ...in two volumes.* London, 1818.

Cotton's *Gleanings*—*Sir Joshua Reynolds and His Works. Gleanings from his Diary, unpublished Manuscripts, and from other Sources. By William Cotton....* London, 1856.

Cotton's *Notes*—*Sir Joshua Reynolds' Notes and Observations on Pictures...edited by William Cotton....* London, 1859.

Leslie and Taylor—*Life and Times of Sir Joshua Reynolds...commenced by Charles Robert Leslie, R.A. continued and concluded by Tom Taylor, M.A. in two volumes.* London, 1865. (The standard biography.)

Graves and Cronin—*A History of the Works of Sir Joshua Reynolds, P.R.A., by Algernon Graves...and William Vine Cronin....* London, 1899–1901. (The four volumes are paged continuously.)

[1] Sir Joshua's existing pocket-books, in which he noted his dinner-engagements and appointments for sitters, are in the Royal Academy, except for the volume for 1755, which is in the Cottonian Collection in the Plymouth Museum. The letters from Mary Palmer to William Johnson were lent, in November, 1925, to Thomas Madigan, Esq., of New York.

BIBLIOGRAPHY

Rutland—The Manuscripts of...the Duke of Rutland (Fourteenth Report of the Hist. MSS. Comm.). Vol. iii, London, 1894; vol. iv, London, 1905.

Gwynn's *Northcote—Memorials of an Eighteenth Century Painter (James Northcote), by Stephen Gwynn.* London, 1898.

Boswell's *Life—Boswell's Life of Johnson...edited by George Birkbeck Hill...in six volumes.* Oxford, 1887.

THE LETTERS

I, II, & III[1]

To the Reverend SAMUEL REYNOLDS

[October, 1740.]

...We see his wife she says she will write to him about it, but I am at present at my Uncle's.[2]...

[December, 1741.]

...on Thursday next, Sir Robert Walpole sits for his picture, master says he has had a great longing to draw his picture, because so many have been drawn, and none like....

[July, 1742.]

...While I am doing this I am the happiest creature alive.[3]...

---

1 From Cotton's *Gleanings*, 47, 50 *et seq*. They are sentences extracted from young Joshua's letters to his father (1681–1745), a Scholar of Corpus Christi College, Oxford, a Fellow of Balliol, and Master of the Plympton School. The approximate dates are determined by the recipient's letters.

2 Joshua had just arrived in London and here refers to his master, Thomas Hudson (1701–1779), the most popular portrait-painter of the day, who was at this time in Bath. The uncle mentioned was probably the Rev. John Reynolds, a Fellow of Eton.

3 *I.e.* while he was painting.

To MISS WESTON

Dear Miss Weston   December o.s. 10th 1749

My Memory is so bad that I vow I dont remember whether or no I writ you about my expedition before I left England, since, I am sure I have not, for I have writ to nobody. I saild from Plimouth so long agone as May 11th[2] and am got no further yet than Port Mahon, but before you shall receive this expect to be on 'tother side the water; I have been kept here near two months by an odd accident, I dont know whether to call it a

1 From the original in my possession. All that is known about the recipient is the romantic story told by John Williams ("Anthony Pasquin") in his *Authentic History of the Professors of Painting... in Ireland*, London (1796), 60, where this and the other two letters to Miss Weston were first published. Briefly, she professed an unrequited love for Sir Joshua, and though "many young Gentlemen paid their addresses" to her, she died unmarried, faithful to him "who, by the suavity of his manners, and the force of his accomplishments, became the point of admiration in those circles in which" she moved. She it was, perhaps, who sat for her portrait on October 20, 1757. Reynolds must have met her some time between 1740 and 1743, during his apprenticeship to Hudson, who, like Miss Weston, lived in Great Queen Street.

2 He had sailed as the guest of the Hon. Augustus Keppel (*cf. post*, Letter XLVIII), then a captain in the navy, who had been appointed commodore of a small squadron which was to carry presents to the Dey of Algiers and to demand restitution of the property taken from the *Prince Frederick*. An account of the trip is given in Northcote, i, 28 *et seq*.

lucky one or not, a fall from a horse down a
precipice, which cut my face in such a manner as
confined me to my room, so that I was forced to
have recourse to painting, [for my a]musement at
first [but have] now finishd as many [pictures as]
will come to a hund[red...] pounds¹ the unlucky
[part of the] Question is my lips are spo[iled for]
kissing for my upper [lip was so] bruisd that a
great p[art was] cut off and the rest [so disfigured]
that I have but a [sorry face] to look at, but in
[time you] wont perceive the d[efect.]

So far it has been t[he best] tour to me that can
[be imagined.] When we were at sea [I occupied]
myself with reading [and made] use of a well
chosen [library of] Books which belong'd to [the
Commodore.² I] was allways in his Cabb[in with
him] and drank with him so that [the whole]
voyage did not cost m[e a penny.] There will be
the more mony you know to spend at the Jubilee.³
Whenever the Commodore went *a shore* at Cadiz
Lisbon Gibralter he allways took me with him and
even when he waited upon the Day or King of
Algiers I went with him and have had the honour
of shaking him by the hand three several times, he

1 The lacunae in the MS. are caused by a part of one of its sides
being torn off. "...before his visit to Italy, his price had been
three guineas a head." (Leslie and Taylor, i, 101 n.)
2 Thus annotated by Reynolds at the bottom of the page:
"Commodore Keppel".
3 1750 was Jubilee year in Rome.

Introduced me likewise to the Governour here General Blackney[1] in so strong a manner that the Governour insisted on my not being at any expence whilst I was on the Island but to eat at his house and orderd his secretary to provide me a lodging. You may imagine I spend my time here very agreably. here are above thirty English Ladies Balls continually at the Generals, and on Board the ships.

When I am settled at Rome I will write to you again to let you know how to direct to me in the mean time I shall be much obliged to you if you will call and see that my Goods are safe and not spoiling I would write to him who has them could I think of his name I should be glad if you had a spare place in your Garret that could they be at your house From your slave

J REYNOLDS

my compliments to M^r. Charlton and M^r. Wilks[2] I hear the whold world is to be at the Jubilee I hope to see Mr Charlton at least there At Lisbon I saw a Bull fight and another at Cadiz which will be the subject of many conversations hereafter

1 William Blakeney (1672–1761), an Irishman of English descent, who first gained fame as Lieutenant-governor of Stirling Castle during the Rebellion of 1745. In 1756 he defended Minorca against the French, gallantly but unsuccessfully.

2 A Mr Charlton appears in his pocket-book for January and August, 1757. "Mr. Wilks" is John, the notorious politician (1727–1797).

6

V[1]

To LORD EDGCUMBE

My Lord,   [1750.]

I am now (thanks to your Lordship) at the height of my wishes, in the midst of the greatest works of art[2] the world has produced. I had a very long passage, though a very pleasant one. I am at last in Rome, having seen many places and sights which I never thought of seeing. I have been at Lisbon, Cadiz, Gibraltar, Algiers, and Mahon. The Commodore staid at Lisbon a week, in which time there happened two of the greatest sights that could be seen had he staid there a whole year—a bull feast, and the procession of *Corpus Christi*. Your Lordship will excuse me if I say, that from the kind treatment and great civilities I have received from the Commodore, I fear I have even laid your Lordship under obligations to him upon my account; since from nothing but your Lordship's recommendation I could possibly expect to meet with that polite behaviour with which I have always been treated: I had the use of his cabin and his study of books as if they had been my own; and when he went ashore, he generally took me with him; so that I not only had an opportunity of

1 From Northcote, i, 34 *et seq.* The recipient, Richard, Baron Edgcumbe of Mount Edgcumbe (1680–1758), had introduced Reynolds to Keppel.
2 In the first edition this word is followed by "that".

7

seeing a great deal, but I saw it with all the advantages as if I had travelled as his equal. At Cadiz I saw another bull feast. I ask your Lordship's pardon for being guilty of that usual piece of ill manners in speaking so much of myself; I should not have committed it after such favours. Impute my not writing to the true reason: I thought it impertinent to write to your Lordship without a proper reason; to let you know where I am, if your Lordship should have any commands here that I am capable of executing. Since I have been in Rome, I have been looking about the palaces for a fit picture of which I might take a copy to present your Lordship with; though it would have been much more genteel to have sent the picture without any previous intimation of it. Any one you choose, the larger the better, as it will have a more grand effect when hung up, and a kind of painting I like more than little. Though[1] it will be too great a presumption to expect it, I must needs own I most impatiently wait for this order from your Lordship.

I am, &c. &c.

JOSHUA REYNOLDS

1 In the first edition this word is followed by "perhaps".

VI[1]

To MISS WESTON

Dear Miss Weston,   [1750.]

I wonder I have not receiv'd an Answer to all the Letters I have sent you this is the third from Rome and one before from Mahon[2] I suppose they have all miscarried so I take this opportunity of sending one by my good Friend M^r. Dalton[3] and a Worthy man he is, I hope he will deliver this Letter himself that you may be acquainted and when I return we shall have many agreeable Jaunts together.

I shall set out from Rome immediatly after the next Lent or Carnival, Give my service to M^r. Charlton and M^r. Wilks and tell them that if it was possible to give them an Idea of what is to be seen here, the Remains of Antiquity the Sculpture, Paintings, Architecture &c., they would think it worth while, nay they would break through all obstacles and set out immediatly for Rome, then

---

1 From the original in the Gratz Collection, in the possession of the Pennsylvania Historical Society. The letter is endorsed in a contemporary hand: "Addressed to Miss Weston of Great Queen St./Lincoln's Inn Fields/ and written at Rome in 1751". I have dated it 1750 because of the reference to "this Jubilee or Holy year".
2 Letter IV in this edition.
3 Richard Dalton (1720–1791), at this time a student of art, later became librarian for George III and first antiquary of the Royal Academy.

9

the Carnival of which I have heard so much that I am resolved to stay here to see the next which they say will exceed all the former since there has been none this Jubilee or Holy year so the next they will make up for the old & the new, If they would set out so as to be here a Month or two before the Carnival after which Ashley[1] and I will accompany them (as we intend to do otherwise) to Venice and from thence to Paris seeing every thing between those two places that are worth seeing going now and then a little out of the direct Road and from thence to England or perhaps we shall go to Antwerp first. I am not in jest now but good earnest and wish they would really think of it M^r. Dalton will acquaint them with the time such a journey will take and the Expence, and the most expeditious way of traveling, I don't think they need be out of England above a year I wish them a good journey if they will write me when they set out I will come as far as Florence to meet them.

send me all the newes you know, not forgetting to say something about my Goods

I am My Dear Miss Weston

Yours

J REYNOLDS

---

1 John Astley (*d.* 1787), portrait-painter, who, like Reynolds, had studied under Hudson. His portrait by Reynolds in black and white chalks on blue paper is in the Print Room of the British Museum.

Don't forget to remember me to M^{rs}. Sutherland, M^r. Hart, and M^r. Price if you ever see them and the M^r. Pines not forgetting the little Girl at Westminster by the Park, write me immediatly immediatly[1] by the first post. M^r. Dalton will tell you how to direct

VII[2]

To MISS WESTON

Dear Miss Weston   Rome. April 30 1751

Your letter I receiv'd with a great [deal] of pleasure and as tis increasing a pleasure to communicate it. I read it to a great many English that were at the Coffe house but without mentioning the writer (tho if I had, it would have been much to your honour) for you must know when a Letter comes from England we are all impatient to hear news, and indeed your Letter whas full of it, and however it happend every person took the same pleasure in it as my self Mr. Lovelace [and] Mrs. Pine were known to most of the painters, others knew Miss Hambleton and others Mr. More. others [the] Miss Gunnings indeed their fame had

1 Perhaps by analogy with "subito subito". I have been unable to identify the persons mentioned, though one of them, perhaps, was William Price, the younger (*d.* 1765), a painter on glass. Robert Edge Pine (1730–1788) and his brother Simon (*d.* 1772), the painters, were probably "the M^r. Pines".

2 From John Williams's *An Authentic History of the Professors of Painting...in Ireland*, London (1796), 63 *et seq.*

reached here some time agone.¹ But nobody but me knew the westminster Girl a lack a lack she has been brought to bed and tis a fine Chumning boy but who is Lord John? well who would have thought it oh the nasty creature to have to do with a man. I am sorry you have been at the expence of paying for my Goods I shall take care to repay you with thanks when I return which will be infallibly this year we set out in about too months time and take the tour of Venice and through Germany and let France alone till next year since it lies so near England that I can take a trip there in a summer and back again my fellow traveller is Mr. Ashley who lived with Mr. Hudson.

We are all extremely afflicted for the loss of the Prince of Whales who certainly would have been a great Patron to Painters as he already was to Mr. Dalton² I feel an additional sorrow on his account I beg my compliments to him particularly and to all friends I ccnnot form to myself any adea of a person more miserable than the Princess of

1 Maria and Elizabeth Gunning, the first of whom became Countess of Coventry and the second Duchess of Hamilton (and of Argyll). They were "declared the handsomest women alive". "The world", wrote Walpole in 1752, "is still mad about the Gunnings". (*Letters of Horace Walpole*, ed. Toynbee, iii, London, 1905, 59, 87.)

2 Frederick-Lewis, father of George III, died March 20, 1751. "It might be imagined this letter was written from Greenland, and not Italy."—Williams. *Cf. ante*, p. 9, n. 3.

Whales must be, deprived at once of a Husband she loved and with him all thoughts of ambition,[1] Adiu I will not desire you to write any Answer to this Letter because I shall remove from Rome to Florence and other Parts of Italy[2] so that you wont know where to direct, but I shall not for that reason neglect writing to you Remember me to mama

Yours

J. REYNOLDS

VIII[3]

To MRS. ELIZABETH HOOPER HUMPHRY

Madam   London April 30th 1765

I am extremely obliged to you for the present you have favourd me with which I am no means entitle'd to, from any civility I may have shewn to your son, his merit in his profession is so great

1 George II had once said of her: "she wants to reign before her time". (Jesse's *George Selwyn and His Contemporaries*, London, 1882, ii, 379.)
2 Actually he remained in Rome until spring of the following year. *V*. Leslie and Taylor, i, 56.
3 From a photostat of the hitherto unpublished original in the library of Haverford College. The letter is addressed: "To M[rs]. Humphrys/at Honiton/near Exeter". The recipient, mother of Ozias Humphry, the miniature-painter, carried on an important business in the Bath Brussels lace industry. She had just sent Reynolds an article of her "own manufacturing". *Cf. post*, Appendix III, Letter A.

13

that a man does honour to himself in recommending him, I have a picture in my possession
of his Painting which is superior to any thing I ever
saw antient or modern,[1] It is with great pleasure
I say this to you who are so nearly interested in his
success

          I am, Madam

             your most humble and

                obedient servant

                       J REYNOLDS

IX[2]

To the DUKE OF NEWCASTLE

          *Leicester fields   Aug 26th 1765

Mr Reynolds presents his duty to His Grace
and will be at Newcastle House tomorrow morning
in order to see the Pictures put in the Frames.

---

1 Perhaps this refers to the copy of "King Lear in the Storm",
which he had considered "superior to anything he had seen in
miniature of modern painting". (Williamson's *Life and Works
of Ozias Humphry*, London, 1918, 24 *et seq.*)
2 From the hitherto unpublished original in the British Museum
(Add. MSS. 32,969, f. 195). Thomas Pelham, Duke of New-
castle-upon-Tyne (1693–1786), was at this time possibly the
most influential figure in English political circles. His name
does not appear in Reynolds's pocket-books.

X[1]

To the Reverend THOMAS PERCY

*Leicester fields April 2d [1768.][2]

Mr. Reynolds presents his Compliments to Mr. Percy and will do himself the honour of waiting on him today at two o clock. Dr. Goldsmith will likewise attend him.

XI[3]

To JOHN JOSHUA KIRBY

Sir   *Leicester Fields, November 25th, 1768.

I beg leave to return my thanks to the gentlemen who have done me the honour of electing me one of the Directors of the Society of Artists. As I have for some years past entirely declined acting as a Director I must now request the favour of

1 From the original in the possession of W. M. Elkins, Esq., of Philadelphia. First published in W. H. Arnold's *Ventures in Book Collecting*, N.Y. 1923, 138.
2 Added by another hand. Reynolds was knighted April 21, 1769.
3 From Whitley's *Artists and their Friends in England—1700–1799*, London, 1928, i, 224. The recipient (1716–1774) had just been elected President of the Incorporated Society of Artists. Reynolds's refusal proceeded partly from his desire to avoid the bitter quarrels of the Society and partly from the fact that plans for the establishment of the Royal Academy were now being drawn up.

15

declining that honour, the doing which I hope will not be understood as proceeding from any want of respect, as I have made the same request to the former set of Directors.

I am, Sir,

Your most humble and obedient Servant

JOSHUA REYNOLDS.

XII[1]

To JAMES BARRY

Dear Sir,   London, [1769.]

I am very much obliged to you for your remembrance of me in your letter to Mr. Burke, which, though I have read with great pleasure, as a composition, I cannot help saying with some regret, to find that so great a portion of your attention has been engaged upon temporary matters,[2] which might be so much more profitably employed upon what would stick by you through your whole life.

Whoever is resolved to excel in painting, or in-

---

1 From *The Works of James Barry, Esq.*, London, 1809, i, 84 *et seq.* The recipient (1741–1806), a protégé of the Burkes, was at this time studying painting in Rome.

2 Barry, whose quarrelsome nature later caused a break with Sir Joshua and eventually expulsion from the Royal Academy, was fighting with picture-dealers in Rome. (*Id.* 75, 114.)

deed any other art, must bring all his mind to bear upon that one object, from the moment he rises till he goes to bed;[1] the effect of every object that meets a painter's eye, may give him a lesson, provided his mind is calm, unembarrassed with other subjects, and open to instruction. This general attention, with other studies connected with the art, which must employ the artist in his closet, will be found sufficient to fill up life, if it was much longer than it is. Were I in your place, I would consider myself as playing a great game,[2] and never suffer the little malice and envy of my rivals to draw off my attention from the main object, which, if you pursue with a steady eye, it will not be in the power of all the Cicerones in the world to hurt you. Whilst they are endeavouring to prevent the gentlemen from employing the young artists, instead of injuring them, they are in my opinion doing them the greatest service. Whilst I was at Rome I was very little employed by them, and that little I always considered as so much time lost: copying those ornamental pictures which the travelling gentlemen always bring home with them as furniture for their houses, is far from

1 Reynolds once told Northcote that "those who were determined to excel must go to work, willing or unwilling, morning, noon, and night". (Gwynn's *Northcote*, 100.) According to Samuel Rogers, he practised what he preached; he "was always thinking of his art". (Leslie and Taylor, ii, 483.)

2 Years later, writing of his early days, he said: "I considered myself as playing a great game". (*Works*, i, p. li.)

being the most profitable manner of a student
spending his time.[1] Whoever has great views,
I would recommend to him whilst at Rome, rather
to live on bread and water than lose those advantages which he can never hope to enjoy a
second time, and which he will find only in the
Vatican, where, I will engage no Cavalier sends
students to copy for him. I do not mean this as any
reproach to the gentlemen; the works in that place,
though they are the proper study of an artist, make
but an aukward figure painted in oil, and reduced
to the size of easel pictures. The Capella Sistina is
the production of the greatest genius that ever was
employed in the arts; it is worth considering by
what principles that stupendous greatness of style
is produced; and endeavouring to produce something of your own on those principles will be a
more advantageous method of study than copying
the St. Cecilia in the Borghese, or the Herodias of
Guido, which may be copied to eternity without
contributing one jot towards making a man a
more able painter.

If you neglect visiting the Vatican often, and
particularly the Capella Sistina, you will neglect
receiving that peculiar advantage which Rome can
give above all other cities in the world. In other
places you will find casts from the antique, and
capital pictures of the great painters, but it is *there*

1 He did, however, offer to copy one for Lord Edgcumbe.
V. ante, p. 8; *cf.* Cotton's *Notes*, 1.

only that you can form an idea of the dignity of the art, as it is there only that you can see the works of Michael Angelo and Raffael. If you should not relish them at first, which may probably be the case, as they have none of those qualities which are captivating at first sight, never cease looking till you feel something like inspiration come over you, till you think every other painter insipid in comparison, and to be admired only for petty excellencies.[1]

I suppose you have heard of the establishment of a royal academy here; the first opportunity I have I will send you the discourse I delivered at its opening, which was the first of January. As I hope you will hereafter be one of our body,[2] I wish you would, as opportunity offers, make memorandums of the regulations of the academies that you may visit in your travels, to be engrafted on our own, if they should be found useful.

I am, with the greatest esteem, yours,

J. REYNOLDS.

---

1 "I remember very well my own disappointment, when I first visited the Vatican.... Notwithstanding my disappointment, I proceeded to copy some of those excellent works.... In a short time a new taste and new perceptions began to dawn upon me; and I was convinced that I had originally formed a false opinion of the perfection of art." (*Works*, i, pp. xiv, xvi.)

2 He was elected an Associate in November, 1772, and was made an Academician the following February.

On reading my letter over, I think it requires some apology for the blunt appearance of a dictatorial style in which I have obtruded my advice. I am forced to write in a great hurry, and have little time for polishing my style.

XIII[1]

To the Hon. WILLIAM HAMILTON

Sir   London, March 28th 1769

I ought to be ashamed to acknowledge the receipt of your kind Letter so many months since, but really my not answering it sooner proceeded rather from a mistake than neglect, your saying I should receive another Letter from you soon I understood to imply that I should delay answering it till I had receiv'd the second, but as no second letter is arrived, I now suspect I was mistaken I hope however you never will think that this delay proceeds from any want of proper attention or that I should be so different from other

---

1 From the hitherto unpublished original in the possession of W. G. Pegg, Esq. of Rothley, Leicestershire. The letter is addressed "A Monsieur/ Monsieur Hamilton/Envoyè extraordinaire/et Plenipotentiaire de S.M. Brit./a Naples ". The recipient (1730–1803), knighted in 1772, in later years became the friend of Nelson and the husband of Emma Hart.

Artists as not to be allways proud of the honour of being remember'd by so great a Patron and judge of Arts as Mr Hamilton.

I admire the work which is publishd under your Patronage exceedingly,[1] it is not only magnificent as it should be, being publishd with your name but it is likewise usefull to antiquarians and will tend to the advancement of the Arts, as adding more materials for Genius to work upon, the grace and genteelness of some of the figures are exquisite, particularly the Atalanta, and it is that kind of grace which I never observed before in the Antique, it is much in the Parmegian stile.

I hope you have been able to pick up some Capital Pictures as well as Etruscan vases. I remember I saw in a Palace at Naples which had but few Pictures, (I think it was that of Franca villa) a small Picture of Paulo Veronese a gre[at] number of figures at Table and Mary Magdalen [washing] Christs feet, I thought it the most

1 *A Collection of Etruscan, Greek, and Roman Antiquities, from the Cabinet of the Honble Wm Hamilton*, etc., by P. F. Hugues (called d'Hancarville). The first volume appeared in 1766, followed in the next year by the other three. F. N. Price, Esq., Keeper of the Greek and Roman Antiquities in the British Museum, has informed me that the design referred to by Sir Joshua and his contemporaries as "Atalanta" has since been proved to be "Castor and Pollux carrying off the daughters of Leukippos". It is on the hydria which is now located in the third vase room of the British Museum (E 224), the same vase which occupies a prominent place in Reynolds's portrait of Sir William which is in the National Portrait Gallery.

To THE HON. WILLIAM HAMILTON   [*1769*

brilliant Pi[cture of] the Master I had ever seen
tho' perhaps they may be too [Rich] to sell it, yet
possibly it may be got at by exchange.[1] I think
it is worth at least a hundred Pounds.

I have the pleasure to acquaint you that the Arts
flourish here with great vigour. we have as good
Artists in every branch of the Art as any other
nation can boast. and the King has very seriously
taken them under his protection, he has establishd
an Academy which opend the first of January.
the Rooms that formerly belonged to Lamb the
Auctioneer in Pall Mall serve for the present till
a proper building can be erected. It would take
up too much room to give you our whole plan,
when it is printed I will take the first opportunity
to send it to you, however I cannot avoid just
giving the outline. It is composed of forty and
cannot exceed that number, out of which are
chosen all the Officers, to the surprise of every
body I have the honour of being President, and it
is only honour for there is no salary annex'd to this
dignity Mr Chambers the Architect is Treasurer
£60 per Ann. Secretary Mr Newton has likewise
£60, The Keeper Mr Moser £100.[2] we have four

1 The lacunae were caused by parts of the MS. sticking to the
seal. Reynolds visited Naples in 1752, but failed to note this
painting in his Journal. *V.* Leslie and Taylor, i, 56 n.
2 William, later Sir William, Chambers, R.A. (1726–1796);
Francis Milner Newton, R.A. (1720–1794); George Michael
Moser, R.A. (1704–1783).

Professors Mr Penny of Painting Mr Chambers of Architecture Mr Wale of Geometry and Perspective and Dr Hunter of Anatomy[1] each gives six Lectures every year—the salery £30 per annum, we have nine Visitors who attend every evening for a month alternately, he must be in the Academy two hours whilst the young men [make] a drawing for which he receives half a Guinea. eight other members are appointed to form the laws, and it is this body which is calld the Councill who govern the Academy, the King interests himself very much in our success he has given an unlimited power to the Tresurer to draw on his Privy Purse for whatever mony shall be wanted for the Academy we have already expended some hundred pounds in purchasing books relating to the Arts. If you should think it proper to mention to the King of Naples the establishment of a Royal Academy he would probably make a present of the Antiquities of Herculaneum.[2]

I am Sir

Yours

J REYNOLDS.

1 Edward Penny, R.A. (1714–1791); Samuel Wale, R.A. (*d.* 1786); William Hunter, M.D., R.A. (1718–1783).
2 Under the auspices of La Reale Accademia Ercolanese di Archeologia were published eight volumes entitled *Le antichità di Ercolano esposte.* The first of these, dealing with painting, appeared in 1757.

23

XIV[1]

To GEORGE AUGUSTUS SELWYN

[March, 1770.]

Sir Joshua Reynolds presents his Compliments to Mr Selwin. The Picture is finished and [he] will send it home tomorrow morning, he has taken the liberty of changing the dress of the head as every person disaproved of it as it stood before.

---

1 From the hitherto unpublished original in the Cely-Trevilian collection, in the possession of the Society of Antiquaries of London. The recipient (1719–1791), wit and politician, apparently sat for his portrait only once after Sir Joshua was knighted. Hence the date inferred.

XV[1]

To NATHANIEL HONE

[April, 1770.]

[The President and Council of the Royal Academy] continue in the same opinion in respect to the cross. They are too dull to see the poignancy of the satire which it conveys.[2] However, were the wit as poignant as you think it, it would be paying too dear for it to sacrifice religion. They confess they have that fear about them of offending against the rules of decency, and have no desire to ridicule religion or make the Cross a subject for buffoonery. You are therefore desired to send for the picture and alter it if you desire to exhibit it this year.

1 From Hodgson and Eaton, *The Royal Academy and its Members*, London, 1905, 33 *et seq*. The original, a rough draft in Sir Joshua's hand, was written just before the opening of the exhibition. The recipient (1718–1784) was an Irish portrait-painter and an Academician.

2 Hone had painted a caricature of two monks carousing, in which there was a crucifix. When the Council objected, he had written: "I should think the poignancy (for I meant it as satire) would lose the best part of its effect".

XVI[1]

To the Hon. WILLIAM HAMILTON

Dear Sir   London June 17th 1770.

I delayed answering your Letter 'till we receiv'd the Casts which you have been so obliging
to give to the Royal Academy, they have been so
long on their passage that we have but just now
receiv'd them. The Basrelievo of Fiamingo I never
saw before it is certainly a very fine group and the
only thing of the kind that we have which makes it
a very acceptable present, that, and the Apollo are
both orderd by his Majesty to be placed in Somerset House where our Academy will remove this
summer,[2] the Royal Apartments are to be con-
verted into a Royal Academy

I beg leave to thank you as President, you will
receive with this an Official Letter of thanks from
the Academy; I must acquaint you that in speaking
to His Majesty some time ago of the Present you had
made and mentioning some other particulars in
the Letter He asked If I had the Letter about me
and if he might see it I had it in my pocket and

---

1 From the hitherto unpublished original in the possession of
C. B. Tinker, Esq.
2 The first meeting of the Academy in Somerset House did not
take place until the following January.

put it in his hands you have no reason to be displeased on any account but there was one circumstance rather fortunate, your having mentiond
His Majesty in it with great affection and certainly
without any expectation of his seeing it. I wonder
he was not tempted by your lively description of
the Corregio,[1] was I King of England I certainly
would have it at all events, there is no Master than
one wishes so much to see. Mr. Aufrere[2] has
brought to England a Marriage of St. Catherine
by Corregio and an undoubted true one, full of
faults and full of Beauties.

I hear that you had the Choice of Lady Betty
Germains Pictures[3] I have no doubt of your
chusing the best. I sent no commision for any
concluding they would all be sold above their
value but the Julio Romano to my great vexation
was sold for fifty Guineas, it is some alleviation that
a person posseses it that knows the value of it Lord
Ossory[4] and I have the pleasure of seeing it very
often.

1 On November 18, 1771, Horace Walpole wrote: "Mr. Hamilton's Correggio is arrived: it is divine", and the following
  month he refers to it as "a charming Correggio". (*Letters*, ed.
  Toynbee, VIII, London, 1904, 107, 118.)
2 George Aufrere (1716–1801), M.P. for Stamford, whose name
  constantly appears in Sir Joshua's pocket-books.
3 Lady Elizabeth Germain (1680–1769), frequently mentioned
  in Swift's *Journal to Stella*, had died December 16.
4 John Fitzpatrick, second Earl of Upper Ossory (1745–1818),
  a close friend and great admirer of Sir Joshua.

27

I beg leave to congratulate you on the honour
you have acquired by the account you have given
to the Royal Society of Vesuvius and Ætna I hear
every[one] speak of it with the highest encomiums
as the [best] account that has hitherto appeared.
I find you are not contented with the reputation
of being at the head of the Virtuosi but are ex-
tending your views to all kinds of knowledge[1]

I dare say you have heard of the report of the
alarm that has been given by our News Papers of
your being cast away in some of your excursions in
hunting for Burning Mountains perhaps the death
of the Elder Pliny put it into somebodys head to
invent the story however I hope you will never
suffer for your eagerness after knowledge but that
you will live and return and be the Mecaenas to
the rising generation of Artists which is the sincere
wish and desire of Sir

Your most humble and obedient servant

JOSHUA REYNOLDS

1 In 1772 was published in London *Observations on Mount Vesuvius,
Mount Etna, and other Volcanos: in a Series of Letters, Addressed to the
Royal Society, From the Honourable Sir W. Hamilton,* etc. The first
four of the six letters had already been written.

XVII[1]

To Sir CHARLES BUNBURY

Dear Sir,   Sep. [7,] 1770.

I have finished the face very much to my own
satisfaction; it has more grace and dignity than
anything I have ever done and it is the best
coloured.[2] As to the dress, I should be glad it
might be left undetermined till I return from my
fortnight's tour, when I return I will try different
dresses. The Eastern dresses are very rich and have
one sort of dignity, but it is a mock dignity in comparison of the simplicity of the antique. The im-

---

1 From Leslie and Taylor, i, 398, altered in accordance with the
part of the text printed in Sotheby's catalogue for a sale,
May 13, 1905 (lot 789). Sir (Thomas) Charles Bunbury (1740–
1821) is frequently mentioned in the correspondence of George
Selwyn. The definite date is derived from Sir Joshua's pocket-
book: "Friday, September 7:—5 o'clock, Sat out for Devonshire".

2 The references are to the portrait of a Miss Kennedy, whose
name is entered in Sir Joshua's pocket-book under date of
January 16. It has not been determined whether she was Polly
Jones, alias Kennedy, a young lady who died in 1781, or Kitty,
the sister of two murderers, Matthew and Patrick Kennedy.
The subject is discussed at length by Horace Bleackley in *Notes
and Queries*, 10 S. vii, 344, ix, 97, and Appendix D of his *Ladies
Fair and Frail*, London, 1909.

patience I have to finish it will shorten my stay in the country.[1] I shall set out in an hour's time.

I am, with the greatest respect,
Your most obliged servant,

J. REYNOLDS.

XVIII[2]

To the Reverend THOMAS PERCY

Dear Sir,   *Leicesterfields, March 3^d [1771].

I am very sorry I engaged myself for to morrow, not an hour ago, I have seen Sig^r. Philippo[3] and admire him very much; I wishd then to take a sketch of him but he went abroad before I had an opportunity.

We shall see you at the Club tomorrow when I hope you will fix a day when we shall have the pleasure of seeing your family in Leicesterfields.

Yours sincerely

JOSHUA REYNOLDS

1 His impatience could not have been very great, since instead of a fortnight's trip to Devonshire, he remained away from London until October 14.

2 From the hitherto unpublished original in the possession of W. M. Elkins, Esq., of Philadelphia. The only year in which Sir Joshua's pocket-books indicate a meeting of the Club for March 4 is 1771.

3 Possibly "an Asiatic" name Phillippo, who had received in 1768 a reward from the Royal Society of Arts for mastering the art of dyeing leather. A happier suggestion is Mr W. T. Whitley's, that this might refer to François André Danican, *dit* Philidor (1727–1795), musician and chess player, who came to England in 1771.

XIX[1]

To —

Sir   Leicesterfields, Aug^st 16 1772

I forgot to ask you when I had the honour of seeing you last about Nancy Reynolds's Picture it is at present in the Possesion of Sir Wm Boothby who would be very glad to keep it.[2] He had it on condition to return it to you if it was demanded if you will please by a line to signify your consent he may then have full possesion of the lady. I take this opportunity of mentioning that I have a small bill on you for your own Picture and the

1 From the hitherto unpublished original in the possession of Goodspeed's Book Shop. I have been unable to identify the recipient.
2 Sir William Boothby (1721–1787), in 1761 Master of the Horse to H.R.H. the Duke of York, was a major-general in the army and colonel of the sixth regiment of foot, who sat to Sir Joshua in 1765. I have been unable to identify Nancy Reynolds, although she is termed "famous" by Leslie and Taylor (ii, 468, n. 8). She seems to have been Sir William's mistress and must have sat for her portrait as early as 1765. Under date of May 20 in that year Sir Joshua has entered in an unpublished account book (now in the Fitzwilliam Museum, Cambridge) the following:

> "Sir Willm. Boothby.............26 5
> D^o for Nancy Reynolds ...25^g...26 5"

The second entry was repeated but crossed out in 1768, and occurs for the last time in 1774 (Cotton's *Notes*, 80, where "26 15 0" is certainly a misprint).

31

$$To \text{———} \qquad [1772$$

Pieta of Palma Giovane   the first was twelve
Guineas the other twenty.

I am, Sir with the greatest respect

your most obedient servant

JOSHUA REYNOLDS

XXI

To PAUL HENRY OURRY, R.N.

Dear Sir   *London Sep 26th 1772.

Yesterday I was informed by a Letter from
Lord Edgcumbe[2] that I have had the honour of
being elected an Alderman of Plympton for which
I beg leave to return, to you in particular, my
most hearty thanks, and must likewise beg the
favour of troubling you to make my acknowledgments to the rest of the Bench. I am sorry it was
not in my power to pay my respects to you this
year and return my thanks in person however
next year I hope to do myself that honour.[3]

---

1 From the original in the Cottonian Collection, in the Municipal
  Museum and Art Gallery, Plymouth. A facsimile faces p. 116
  of Cotton's *Gleanings*. The recipient, at this time a captain, later
  became an admiral. In 1780 he was M.P. for Plympton.
2 George, Baron Edgcumbe of Mount Edgcumbe (1720–1795),
  later Earl of Mount Edgcumbe.
3 His pocket-book shows that in the following year, while visiting
  in Devonshire, he dined with "Oury" on September 27.

I beg my compliments to M^rs. Ouray, Miss and
all your family and am with the greatest respect
Sir
Your most humble
and obliged servant
JOSHUA REYNOLDS

XXI^1

To MRS. ELIZABETH ROBINSON MONTAGU

Madam   [March–April, 1773]

M^r. Burk spoke of M^r. Vesey^2 when he proposed him last Friday^3 in the same manner as you
have done, and I think in the very words, that he

1 From a photostat of the original in the Henry E. Huntington
  Library and Art Gallery. First published in Reginald Blunt's
  Mrs. Montagu: Her Letters and Friendships, London, 1924, ii, 10.
  The recipient (1720–1800) was the originator of "The Blue
  Stocking Club".
2 Agmondisham Vesey, now chiefly known as husband of a
  famous bluestocking, was elected to the Club on April 2, from
  which is deduced the approximate date of the letter. "When
  Mr. Vesey was proposed as a member of the LITERARY
  CLUB, Mr. Burke began by saying that he was a man of gentle
  manners. 'Sir, said Johnson, you need say no more. When you
  have said a man of gentle manners; you have said enough.'"
  (Boswell's *Life*, iv, 28.) Six years later, Malone, who was a
  candidate for election, wrote to Lord Charlemont: "I am not
  quite so anxious as Agmondesham Vesey was, who I am told,
  had couriers stationed to bring him the quickest intelligence of
  his success". (*Hist. MSS. Comm.* XII, 1891, *Charlemont*, i, 344.)
3 March 26.

was good humoured sensible, well bred, and had all the social virtues; it was left for you to say that he was a man of Tast without pretensions and so without jealousy and envy. I have too good an opinion of our club to entertain the least suspicion that such a man will not be unanimously elected.

I have every reason to wish M^r. Vesey success but for none more than your interesting yourself in his favour. and tho' I am very much flatterd by your applying to me in this affair, you may depend on my religiously observing your injunction[1]

I am with the greatest respect

Madam

your most humble

and obliged servant

JOSHUA REYNOLDS

P S. M^r. Cumberland[2] is not a member of the Club.

1 Possibly she had requested him not to mention her name in connection with Vesey's election, lest she be accused of meddling in what was none of her business.
2 Richard Cumberland (1732–1811), the dramatist. "They never admitted C—— as one of the set; Sir Joshua did not invite him to dinner." (Hazlitt's *Conversations of James Northcote*, London, 1830, 275.)

XXII[1]

To the Right Hon. LUKE GARDINER

Sir,   [July, 1773.]

I intended long ago to have returned you
thanks for the agreeable employment in which you
have engaged me, and likewise for the very obliging manner in which this favour was conferred;
but immediately after the heads were finished,
I was enticed away to Portsmouth, and from thence
to Oxford, from whence I am but just returned;[2]
so that this is the first quiet minute I have had for
this month past; though it is a little delayed by
these holidays, it will not, upon the whole, fare
the worse for it, as I am returned with a very keen
appetite to the work. This picture is the great
object of my mind at present. You have been

---

1 From Northcote, i, 292 *et seq*. The recipient (1745–1798), M.P.
for co. Dublin and member of the Privy Council in Ireland, had
married on July 3 Elizabeth, eldest daughter of Sir William
Montgomery, Bart. On May 27 he had written Sir Joshua,
requesting in a flattering note that he "compose a picture" of
his fiancée and her two sisters, Anne, Viscountess Townshend,
and the Hon. Mrs Beresford. He wished "to have their portraits
together at full length, representing some emblematical or
historical subject". (Northcote, i, 291.)
2 For the diary of his trip to Portsmouth see Leslie and Taylor,
ii, 27 n. From July 6 to 14 he had been in Oxford, where he
had received the honorary degree of D.C.L. Sittings had begun
on June 7 and continued until November. The picture, now
in the National Gallery, was exhibited the following spring.

already informed, I have no doubt, of the subject which we have chosen; the adorning a Term of Hymen with festoons of flowers. This affords sufficient employment to the figures, and gives an opportunity of introducing a variety of graceful historical attitudes. I have every inducement to exert myself on this occasion, both from the confidence you have placed in me, and from the subjects you have presented to me, which are such as I am never likely to meet with again as long as I live, and I flatter myself that, however inferior the picture may be to what I wish it, or what it ought, it will be the best picture I ever painted. I beg leave to congratulate you and Mrs. Gardiner,[1] and express my sincere wishes for that perfect happiness to which you are both so well intitled.

I am, with great respect, &c.

JOSHUA REYNOLDS

I shall send away your picture (the best of the two) immediately; the other I know is to remain here. I have forgot to what place it is to be sent.[2]

---

1 Northcote gives "Mrs. G——."
2 The postscript casts doubt on the conclusions of Graves and Cronin (345 *et seq.*). It would seem that Taylor (ii, 5) was correct in assuming that it was Luke Gardiner, not his brother, who was sitting for his portrait in March of this year.

XXIII[1]

To LORD HARDWICKE

My Lord   London Oct. 16. 1773.

I was out of Town when your Lordships note arrived[2] or I should have answered it immediatly. Mr Pars[3] says the Picture of the Lake of Como will be quite finished in a weeks time when he will send it as directed to St. James' Square. The price will be the same as that which was in the Exhibition which was eight Guineas.

I fear our scheme of ornamenting St Paul's with Pictures is at an end. I have heard that it is disaproved off by the Archbishop of Canterbury and by the Bishop of London.[4] For the sake of the advantage which would accrue to the Arts by establishing a fashon of having Pictures in Churches, six Painters[5] agreed to give each of them a Picture to St. Pauls which were to be placed in that part

1 From the original in the British Museum (Add. MSS. 35,350, f. 47). A facsimile appears as no. 27 in series 5 of *Facsimiles of ...Autographs in the...British Museum*, ed. Warner, London, 1899. The recipient was Philip Yorke, second Earl of Hardwicke (1720–1790).

2 He had been in Plympton, where he was sworn in as mayor.

3 William Pars, A.R.A. (1742–1782), who had exhibited in this year "A view on the lake of Como".

4 The Hon. Frederick Cornwallis (1713–1783) was Archbishop of Canterbury from 1768 until his death. From 1764 until 1777 the Bishop of London was Richard Terrick.

5 Reynolds, West, Barry, Dance, Cipriani, and Angelica Kauffman. A complete account of this affair is given in Northcote, i, 305 *et seq.*

37

of the Building which supports, the Cupola & which was intended by Sir Christoph[er] Wren to be ornamented either with Pictures or Bas reliefs as appears from his Drawings. The Dean of St. Paul[1] and all the Chapter are very desirous of this scheme being carried into execution but it is uncertain whether they will be able to prevail on those two great Prelates to comply with their wishes.   I am with the greatest respect

Your Lordships most humble
and obedient servant.

JOSHUA REYNOLDS

XXIV[2]

To BENJAMIN WEST

[1773.]

Sir Joshua Reynolds presents his Compliments and begs to know if Mr West can inform him where Mr G. Hamilton's Prints are to be sold.[3]

1 Thomas Newton (1704–1782), Bishop of Bristol and Dean of St. Paul's, who had approached the various guardians of the cathedral without success. While in Bristol in the previous month, Sir Joshua had dined with him.

2 From Catalogue 492 (Sept. 1901) issued by Walter V. Daniell, of London. The recipient (1738–1820) was a foundation member of the Royal Academy and later succeeded Sir Joshua as its president.

3 In 1773 Gavin Hamilton (1730–1813), historical painter, published in Rome a folio entitled *Schola Italica Picturae, sive selectae quaedam summorum e schola Italica pictorum tabulae aere incisae cura et impensis Gavini Hamilton pictoris.*

To JAMES BEATTIE

London, 22d February, 1774.

I sit down to relieve my mind from great anxiety and uneasiness, and I am very serious when I say, that this proceeds from not answering your letter sooner. This seems very strange, you will say, since the cause may be so easily removed; but the truth of the matter is, I waited to be able to inform you that your picture was finished, which, however, I cannot now do. I must confess to you, that when I sat down, I did intend to tell a sort of a white lie, that it was finished: but on recollecting that I was writing to the author of truth, about a picture of truth,[2] I felt that I ought to say nothing but truth. The truth then is, that the picture probably will be finished, before you receive this letter; for there is not above a day's work remaining to be done. Mr. Hume[3] has heard from somebody, that he is introduced in the picture, not much to his

1 From Sir William Forbes's *Life and Writings of James Beattie*, Edinburgh, 1806, i, 331 *et seq.* The recipient (1735–1803), philosopher and poet, had sat for his portrait in August.

2 In the picture Beattie, as champion of Truth, is holding in his hands a copy of his *Essay on Truth* (published in 1770), which had been directed against Hume's *Infidelity*.

3 David Hume (1711–1776), historian and sceptic. " ... a female personification of Truth is driving down to perdition three demons, one of which resembles Voltaire, and the others, it has been said, Hume and Gibbon." (Leslie and Taylor, ii, 30.)

credit; there is only a figure covering his face with his hands, which they may call Hume, or any body else; it is true it has a tolerable broad back. As for Voltaire, I intended he should be one of the group.

I intended to write more, but I hear the post-man's bell. Dr. Johnson, who is with me now, desires his compliments.

XXVI[1]

To DAVID GARRICK

Dear Sir,   Leicester-fields, August 2, 1774.

The connexion which I have with the author of the tragedy which accompanies this, makes it impossible for me to refuse him the favour of pre-senting it to you.[2] I shall take it as a great [favour] if you will take the trouble of reading it, and give your opinion of it, if it will do.

I should not take this liberty if I was not in some

---

1 From *The Private Correspondence of David Garrick*, London, 1831, i, 646, altered in accordance with the part of the text given in facsimile in *Lettres Autographes. . de M. Alfred Bovet*, ed. Charavay, Paris, 1885, facing p. 676. The original is in the possession of R. B. Adam, Esq., of Buffalo.

2 Sir Joshua's nephew, Joseph Palmer (1749–1829), had written a tragedy entitled *Zaphira*. Garrick's notes on it, now in the Forster MSS. in the Victoria and Albert Museum, are printed in his *Private Correspondence, loc. cit.* "The tragedy, even with some alterations and shortenings, is not likely to succeed, as it wants a great and interesting scene in the last act."

measure authorised by the approbation of Ed^d.
Burk and Johnson   The latter contrary to his
custom read it quite through.[1]

The Author will very readily make any alterations that may be suggested to him

I am Dear Sir

with the greatest respect

yours

JOSHUA REYNOLDS

XXVII[2]

To DAVID GARRICK

Dear Sir,   Leicester-fields, Sept. 4th, 1774.

I thought of delaying to answer your note
till I should hear from the author, who is in the
country;[3] but on second thoughts it must needs
be altogether unnecessary to give you the trouble

1 In the previous year "Mr. Elphinston talked of a new book that
was much admired, and asked Dr. Johnson if he had read it.
JOHNSON. 'I have looked into it.' 'What (said Elphinston,)
have you not read it through?' Johnson, offended at being
thus pressed, and so obliged to own his cursory mode of reading,
answered tartly, 'No, Sir, do *you* read books *through*?'" (Boswell's *Life*, ii, 226.)
2 From *The Private Correspondence of David Garrick*, i, 658. The
original was sold at the Anderson Galleries, March 14, 1921,
to F. G. Miller, Esq.
3 According to Leslie and Taylor (ii, 88) he was with his family
in Torrington.

of reading the play, as you say it cannot be acted, even if you should approve of it, for these two years to come. He will undoubtedly understand your answer to be an absolute refusal to take it at any rate; I must, therefore, beg that it may be returned.

I am, with great respect,

Your most humble and obedient servant,

JOSHUA REYNOLDS

XXVIII[2]

To DAVID GARRICK

Dear Sir,   Leicester-fields, Sept. 9th, 1774.

I confess to you I could not conceive that you could possibly be engaged for two years to come, and thought I ought to understand it as a refusal; but I am now perfectly satisfied that I was mistaken.[2] At any rate, to make use of the same

1 From *The Private Correspondence of David Garrick*, ii, 2. The original was sold at Sotheby's July 7, 1921, to the Messrs Maggs.
2 Garrick had written to him on September 5: "I have no less than seven plays, each of five acts, and two smaller pieces for representation; these, with our revised plays, will be as much as any manager can thrust with all his might into two seasons". (*Op. cit.* i, 658.) The editor shows, however, that Garrick was not entirely honest in this instance.

expression,[1] any appearance of solicitude from Mr. Garrick that there should be no misunderstanding, is very flattering to his sincere friend and admirer,   JOSHUA REYNOLDS

XXIX[2]

To the Reverend THOMAS PERCY

*Leicesterfields March 1ˢᵗ [1775.][3]

Sir Joshua Reynolds presents his Compliments to Dʳ. Percy

That Her Grace[4] may be sure of having the very best Impression he has sent the Print which the Engraver gave him and will get another for himself

he finds by looking in his Book that he is engaged next Wednesday, any day after that that you will appoint

---

1 The penultimate sentence in Letter XXVII ends with the words "at any rate". Garrick had repeated this phrase in the answer referred to above.

2 From the hitherto unpublished original in the possession of W. M. Elkins, Esq., of Philadelphia.

3 The letter must be dated between 1769, when Percy received his degree of D.D. from Cambridge, and 1776, when the Duchess of Northumberland died. If the engraving here referred to is that of Reynolds's portrait of Percy (engraved 1775), the date adopted is probably correct.

4 Elizabeth, Duchess of Northumberland (1716–1776), to whom Percy had dedicated his *Reliques* in 1764. For her interest in prints see Gaussen's *Percy: Prelate and Poet*, London, 1908, 131.

XXX[1]

To CALEB WHITEFOORD

*Leicester fields   April 15th [1775.]

Sir Joshua Reynolds presents his Compliments to Mr Whitford If he has no objection [he] should be glad to send his Picture to the Exhibition[2]

XXXI[3]

To CALEB WHITEFOORD

*Sunday [April 23 (?), 1775.][4]

The scheme of hanging the Pictures Numerically is frustrated from the Information the

1 From the hitherto unpublished original in the British Museum. (Add. MSS. 36,595, f. 206.) The recipient (1734–1810) was the wine-merchant whom Goldsmith described as "Rare compound of oddity, frolic, and fun!/Who relish'd a joke, and rejoic'd in a pun". He later became one of the plenipotentiaries sent to Paris to arrange the terms of peace after the American Revolution.
2 Whitefoord's portrait, which had been begun December 2, 1773, was paid for the following October and was exhibited in 1775.
3 From the original in the British Museum (Add. MSS. 36,595, ff. 204–5). First published in Whitley's *Artists and their Friends in England*, London, 1928, i, 320 *et seq.*
4 The approximate date derives from a letter published Wednesday, April 19, in the *Public Advertiser*, in which the correspondent

Printer[1] has given us that—after he has receiv'd
the Copy of the Catalogue it will take a whole
week in Printing, this is more time time than we
can afford—for the Catalogue cannot be written
till all the Pictures are hung up and number'd—
when the Council adopted the scheme they
thought two days were sufficient for the Printing—
Pray ask Mr. Woodfall[2] if he could undertake to
deliver us half a dozen Impression[s] within eight
& forty hours after he has receiv'd the Copy—
I have sent an old Catalogue for him to see about
what quantity of Printing is required

Yours sincerly

J REYNOLDS

(possibly Whitefoord) suggested that the pictures in the Exhibition should be numbered consecutively after they had been
hung, and that the catalogue should then be printed to agree
with this numeration. The suggestion was not adopted until
1780.

1 William Griffin, printer to the Academy from November, 1769,
until June, 1775.

2 Henry Sampson Woodfall (1739–1805), printer of the *Public
Advertiser* and the letters of Junius. He was a close friend of
Whitefoord. *V. The Whitefoord Papers*, ed. Hewins, Oxford,
1898, 155, 161.

XXXII[1]

To Sir JOHN PRINGLE

Leicester-fields, Oct. 4, 1775.

Sir Joshua Reynolds presents his compliments to Sir John Pringle: he has been searching for prints of his uncle,[2] but can find but one, which he has sent him. The plate, he has been informed, is in the hands of Mr. Sayer, print-seller, in Fleet-street, who bought, after McArdell's death, most of his plates. He is very glad to find that his uncle's name will be perpetuated in Mr. Granger's History,[3] and is sorry he cannot furnish him with more of his prints.

1 From *The Letters of James Granger*, London, 1805, 52. The recipient (1707–1782) was president of the Royal Society and physician to the King.
2 The Rev. John Reynolds (1671–1758), Fellow of Eton and King's College, Cambridge, and Canon of St Peter's, Exeter. The print referred to had been made from Sir Joshua's portrait by James MacArdell (1729?–1765), mezzotint-engraver.
3 In 1769 the Rev. James Granger (1723–1776) had brought out *A Biographical History of England*, etc., a work which gives brief biographies of illustrious Englishmen, as well as information about engravings of their portraits. His death the year after this letter was written accounts for the fact that Reynolds is not included in subsequent editions.

XXXIII[1]
To [Dr. SAMUEL FARR.]

Dear Sir   *Leicester fields   Nov 23 1775

I beg leave to reccommend to your protection Mr. Waldre[2] a very ingenious Artist who intends to succeed Mr Poggi,[3] and I hope under yours and Mr. Mudges[4] Patronage he will meet with equal success both in the School of Drawing, and in the school of Love and carry off triumphantly a fine young Lady with a good Fortune

I beg my Compliments [to] Mrs. Farr and my little sweetheart

I am with the greatest respect

your most humble

and obedient servant

JOSHUA REYNOLDS

1 From the hitherto unpublished original in the Cely-Trevilian collection, in the possession of the Society of Antiquaries of London. The recipient was probably Samuel Farr (1741–1795), physician, a native of Taunton, with whom Sir Joshua notes in his pocket-books dinner engagements for October 1, 1773, and June 8, 1779.

2 Vincent Waldré, decorative painter, who married, not in Devonshire, but in Ireland, where he proceeded in 1787.

3 Anthony Poggi, portrait painter, who exhibited at the Royal Academy from 1776 to 1781. He had up to this time been painting in Plymouth. *Cf.* Whitley's *Artists and their Friends in England*, ii, 300.

4 Thomas Mudge (1717–1794), horologist, an old friend of Sir Joshua's, who had moved to Plymouth in 1771.

XXXIV[1]

To GIUSEPPE PELLI

Di Londra, 26 Gennajo, 1776
Signior Pelli mio,

Non che in Italiano, io non saprei nè tampoco
esprimervi in Inglese il piacere cagionato mi dalla
vostra pulitissima Lettera, che mi dice come il mio
Ritratto s' ha ottenuto il compatimento del Signor
Arciduca Granduca,[2] che ha pur nome d'intendersi
tanto d'opere di pennello, quanto d'ogn' altra bella
cosa.

Io sono infinitamente obbligato alla sua gene-
rosità tutta reale, non solo per essersi degnato d'
ammettermi in quella sua unica maravigliosissima
stanza, quanto anche per avermi in quella segnato
l' onorevole luogo da voi mentovatomi. Quanto

1 From *The Athenaeum* for July 25, 1874 (p. 119), a reference
kindly supplied by Mr W. T. Whitley. Leslie and Taylor, ii,
165 *et seq.*, print the rough draft and add an English translation.
The letter is addressed: "All' Illustrissimo Signore, Il Signore
Giuseppe Pelli,/Direttore della Reale Galleria, Firenze./A
Monsieur,/Monsieur Louis Siries, à Florence, Italy". Besides
being Director of the Royal Gallery, the recipient (1729–1808)
was secretary to the Archduke.
2 Sir Joshua, when elected to the Academy at Florence, had presented his portrait to Archduke Leopold (1747–1792), later
King of the Romans. Pelli's "pulitissima lettera", written at
Florence November 21, 1775, makes it possible to give an
approximate date for Sir Joshua's answer. *Cf. post*, Appendix
III, Letter D.

48

aveva ragione di pavoneggiarmi, se potessi ritornare
a veder l' Italia, e a riconoschermi, un tratto in
mezzo a quegl' illustri Eroì dell' arte che professo?
Se quoque principibus permixtum agnovit Achivis.[1] Come
chè, a dir vero, l' età del viaggiare mi sia oggimai
passata, pure non posso impedirmi dal rallegrare fre-
quenti volte la mia mente col pensiero di trovarmi
costà. E il mio desiderio di rivedere la vostra bella
Firenze, ben potete credere, Signor Pelli, che sia
ora cresciuto a molti doppi, essendo ora in certo
modo legato e connesso con voi, e divenuto in
qualche foggia come un vostro concittadino. Ora
sì, che mi chiamo pienamente pagato del mio
vigoroso raccomandare negli annuali miei Ragio-
namenti alla nostra Accademia il merito altissimo
del divino vostro Michelagnolo,[2] sempre offren-
dolo non solo come principale, ma come unico
modello a tutti coloro che in essa coltivano l' arti
del Disegno; e questa fù una delle ragioni che mi
fecero accennare nel Ritratto, quello che ho tante
volte inculcato colle parole. Nè con questo ho io
mai inteso di accrescere onore a quel sublime
uomo, ma sibbene mostrare nella mia patria che
ho almeno discernimento uguale all obbligo ap-
pogiatomi di consigliare de' discepoli, e che so
metterli sulla vera strada della perfezione.

Non mi rimane ora che a ringraziare voi pure

1 *Aeneid,* 1, 488.
2 Michelagnolo had been mentioned in every *Discourse* but the
third.

del molto sconcio da voi preso per favorirmi senz'
alcuno mio previo merito, e pregarvi di qualche
vostro comando, onde possa mostrarvi, che la mia
riconoscenza non è minore di quel rispetto, con
cui mi farò sempre mai onore di sottoscrivermi.

Signor mio stimatissimo,

Vostro servo e leale servidore,

JOSHUA REYNOLDS.

XXXV[1]

To GIUSEPPE PELLI

Di Londra, 13 Luglio, 1776.

Ornatissimo Signor Pelli,

Avrei prima d' ora risposto alla vostra non
meno elegante che gentile de' 25 Marzo passato;
se non avessi aspettato le Medaglie[2] un dì dopo
l' altro. Finalmente le sono venute, ed Io non posso
far altro che ringraziare colla più ossequiosa riconoscenza il Real donatore, che ha così degnato
di contribuire allo accrescimento del mio buon
nome fra i Professori delle bell' arti. Compiace-
tevi, Signor mio stimatissimo, di esprimere la mia
somma gratitudine all' Altezza sua tanto magna-
nima, e colle più vive parole che potrete, assi

1 From *The Athenaeum* for July 25, 1874 (p. 119). A slightly
abbreviated translation appears in Whitley's *Artists and their
Friends in England*, i, 315.
2 In return for Sir Joshua's portrait the Archduke had sent him
these medals. *Cf. post*, Letter CXLI.

50

curandola che farò quanto potrò per chè questo
pegno della sua somma bontà e condiscendenza
venga un pezzo conservato nella mia famiglia,
onde possa pure lungamente conservarsi in essa
la divozione verso il mio munificente benefattore.

Vossignoria poi, Signo Pelli mio, si compiaccia
di pensare a darmi qualche modo di poter le
mostrare quanto le sono obbligato pel lungo in-
comodo che s' ha preso in favorirmi, e non voglio
che la nostra ben cominciata corrispondenza ed
amicizia finisca sì tosto, protestandole con tutta
la sincerità e con tutto il respetto possibile, che
desidero molto ardentamente di mostrarmi a tutte
prove.

Di Vossignoria stimatissima,

Umilissimo ed affezionatiss

Servidore,

JOSHUA REYNOLDS.

XXXVI[1]

To JAMES NORTHCOTE

Deer Sir   London Sep. 3, 1776

I am very much obliged to you for your kind
remembrance of me and am very glad to hear of

[1] From a facsimile facing p. 1 of Northcote, ii. The recipient
(1746–1831), Sir Joshua's pupil and biographer, had left him
on May 12 after having studied under him for five years, and
had gone to Portsmouth, where he had painted a number of
portraits. "From Portsmouth I wrote a letter to my friend, Sir
Joshua Reynolds, acquainting him of my success." (Gwynn's
Northcote, 115.)

your great success, which you very well deserve, and I have no doubt but you will meet with the same encouragement when you come to settle in London which I hope you do not forget. Here is the place where you must think of setting up your stuff[1] after you have made a short trip (at least) to Italy which your success at Portsmouth and Plimouth will enable you to accomplish[2] If I can ever be of any service to you you know you may command me   I am dear Sir

Yours sincerely

JOSHUA REYNOLDS

I beg when you write to Mrs Northcote[3] you would thank her for her present

XXXVII[4]

To —

Dear Sir   March 5th 1777

I have receiv'd the inclosed from Mrs Burk[5] I need not say how much I wish to oblige Mrs

1 Northcote gives "yourself". (Gwynn, *op. cit.* 116.) Mr L. F. Powell, to whom I am indebted for helpful criticism, suggests "your staff".
2 He left for Italy at the end of the following March.
3 The recipient's mother, who lived in Plymouth.
4 From a copy of the hitherto unpublished original in the possession of M. H. Spielmann, Esq., of Uplands, Folkestone.
5 Probably Jane Nugent, wife of Edmund Burke. I have taken the liberty of reading *Burk* for *Busk*. Though Mr Spielmann believes Sir Joshua "could hardly have mis-spelt the name of a man whom he knew so well", I have been able to find but one

Burk and as I know you have the same wishes towards that family I have no doubt you will use
your Interests to procure what she desires

Yours sincerely

J REYNOLDS

XXXVIII[1]
To HARRY VERELST

*Leicester fields July 7th 1777

Sir Joshua Reynolds presents his Compliments to Mr Vareilst and returns him many thanks
for having indulged him with a sight of the Indian
Drawings, many of which he thinks admirable
particularly the half dozen which he placed in the
beginning of the book.[2]

He begs leave to make his apology for not knowing that it was from Mr Vereilst himself he receivd it.

instance, in the original letters I have seen, in which the name is
correctly spelt. (Letter LXXX; *cf.* Letters XXI and XXVI.) In his
pocket-books Reynolds almost invariably uses the shorter form;
between the years 1764 and 1781 I have noted twenty-eight
entries of his name, only one of which is properly spelt; during
the same period his wife's name appears ten times, always as
Mrs. Burk. Cf. post, Appendix III, Letter R.

1 From the hitherto unpublished original in the possession of the
Messrs Maggs. The recipient (*d.* 1785), Governor of Bengal
from 1767 to 1769, was the grandson of Cornelius Verelst,
flower-painter, and had been brought up by his uncle, Willem
Verelst, portrait-painter.

2 At the bottom of the note Sir Joshua has added the following
six numbers: "28, 40, 30, 27, 20, 21".

XXXIX[1]

To THEOPHILA PALMER

Leicester Fields, August 12, 1777

My dear Offee,

I set out to-morrow for Blenheim.[2] I had some thoughts of bringing you to town, as it coincided with a very pressing invitation which I had from Lord Granby[3] to pass some days at Chiveley, but, receiving at the same time a letter that I was expected at Blenheim, that scheme is at an end, and how you will come to town the Lord knows. In regard to our separation, I feel exactly as you have expressed yourself. You say you are perfectly happy where you are from the kindness and civility of your hostess and Miss Horneck,[4] and

1 From Leslie and Taylor, ii, 317 n. The original is in the possession of the recipient's great-grandson, R. G. Gwatkin, Esq., of Potterne, Devizes. It is addressed: "Miss Palmer, at Mrs. Bunbury's, Barton, near Bury, Suffolk". The recipient (1757–1843), one of Sir Joshua's nieces, lived with him, with the exception of a few years, from October, 1770, until her marriage. *Cf. post*, Letter LV.
2 Where he remained until September 4, completing his great picture of the Marlborough family.
3 Charles Manners (1754–1787), later fourth Duke of Rutland. *Cf. post*, p. 96, n. 3.
4 Her hostess was Catherine Horneck (Goldsmith's "Little Comedy"), who had married in 1771 Henry William Bunbury, the artist. "Miss Horneck" was her sister Mary ("the Jessamy Bride"), later the wife of Col. Gwyn.

54

only wish to see us. We wish likewise to see you, at the same time that we are perfectly well contented with your absence, when it is in a family which will somewhat contribute to confirm, by habit, those principles in which you have been educated, which habits I have always thought are infinitely beyond all precepts, which go into one ear and out at the other. I never was a great friend to the efficacy of precept, nor a great professor of love and affection, and therefore I never told you how much I loved you, for fear you should grow saucy upon it.

I have got a ring and a bracelet of my own picture; don't you tell your sister that I have given you your choice.[1]

My compliments to all the family, and remain,

Dear Offee,

Your affectionate Uncle,

J. REYNOLDS

---

1 I assume that he refers to the portrait painted for the gallery in Florence (*v. ante*, Letter xxxiv), which had been engraved this year. Offy's sister Mary (1750–1820), later Marchioness of Thomond, lived with Sir Joshua from October, 1773, until his death, with the exception of three years.

XL[1]

To DANIEL DAULBY

*London Sep 9th 1777

I am just returnd from Blenheim[2] consequently did not see your Letter till yesterday as they neglected sending it to me—My prizes—for a head is thirty five Guineas—As far as the Knees seventy—and for a whole-length one hundred and fifty.

It requires in general three sittings about an hour and half each time but if the sitter chooses it the face could be begun and finished in one day it is divided into seperate times for the convenience and ease of the person who sits, when the face is finished the rest is done without troubling the sitter.

I have no picture of the kind you mention by me, when I paint any picture of invention it is allways engaged before it is half finished.

---

1 From the hitherto unpublished original in the Fitzwilliam Museum, Cambridge. It is addressed: "To M[r]. Daulby/to the care of M[r]. W[m]. Roscoe/ Lord Street/Liverpool". The recipient (*d.* 1797), brother-in-law of William Roscoe (*v. post*, Letter LXXVIII), was never painted by Sir Joshua. He owned a "complete and valuable collection of the prints of Rembrandt". (Roscoe's *Life of William Roscoe*, London, 1833, i, 215, 226.)
2 *V. ante*, p. 54, n. 2.

I beg leave to return my thanks for the favourable opinion you entertain of me and am with the greatest respect

Your most obedient

humble Servant

JOSHUA REYNOLDS

XLI[1]

To SAMUEL JOHNSON

Dear Sir,   [Dec. 17th, 1777.]

I am making additions and should wish you to see it all together. If I sent it to you now, I must send it again when those additions are finished, I have not courage enough to appear in public without your imprimatur.

I am very much obliged to you for thinking about it, on Friday next I hope to send to Southwark.[2]

Yours most affectionately, etc.

1 From Sotheby's catalogue for a sale held February 5, 1920. The date is given in Sotheby's catalogue for a sale held June 17, 1899. The year is conjectural. The letter unquestionably refers to Sir Joshua's *Discourses*, the first of which was delivered January 2, 1769, and succeeding ones usually on December 10. I have selected 1777, because at this time Sir Joshua was revising them for the first collected edition, in which the dedication to the King was written by Johnson. (Boswell's *Life*, ii, 2 n.)

2 From about 1765 to about the end of 1780 Johnson had "an apartment" in Thrale's house at Southwark. (Boswell's *Life*, iii, 406 n.)

57

XLII[1]

To the Reverend JOHN OGLANDER

Sir   Leicesterfields Dec 27 1777

I am extremely glad to hear the Society have determined to place all our works together in the West window to make one complete whole, insteed of being distributed in different parts of the Chapel. In my conversation with Mr Jervais[2] about it he thought it might be possible to change the Stone work of the window so as to make a principal predominant space in the Centre without which it will be difficult to produce a great effect, as M^r. Jervais is now at Oxford I need add no more, I have allready expressd to him how much I wishd this alteration might be practicable

I am with the greatest respect
your most obedient servant

JOSHUA REYNOLDS

1 From the original presented to New College, Oxford, by Cecil Harmsworth, Esq. It was through the efforts of Mrs Rowell, of Johnson's House in Gough Square, that this letter was located for me. First published by Malone (*Works*, i, p. lix). The recipient (1737–1794) was Warden of New College.
2 Thomas Jervais (*d.* 1799), glass-painter, whose most famous work was copying Sir Joshua's designs for the west window of New College, which forms the subject of this and the following letter.

58

XLIII[1]

To the Reverend JOHN OGLANDER

Dear Sir   London Jan. 9th 1778

I have inclosed a drawing[2] copied from that
which was sent to Mr. Jervais, leaving out what
I wish to be removed, by this you will see that
I have changed the first intention which regarded
the lower tier of the divisions of windows to that of
making the large space, in the centre; The advantage the window receives from this change is
so apparent at first sight that I need not add the
authority and approbation of Sir Wm. Chambers to
persuade you to adopt it, indeed not only Sir
Willm. but every person to whom I have shewn it
approve[s] of the alteration Mr. T. Warton[3]
amongst the rest thinks the beauty of the window
will be much improved supposing the Pictures
which are occupy[ing] the space out of the question. This change by no means weakens the
window, the stone pillars which are removed,

1 From the original in the possession of Oliver R. Barrett, Esq.,
   of Chicago. Partly published by Malone (*Works*, i, pp. lix *et
   seq.*).
2 This diagram of the proposed alterations in the divisions of the
   window is also in Mr Barrett's possession.
3 Thomas Warton (1728–1790), historian of English poetry
   (*v. post*, Letter LXII). For Sir William Chambers, *v. ante*,
   p. 22.

59

suppo[r]ting only the ornament[s] above   which are removed with it.

Supposing this scheme to take place my Idea is to paint in the great space in the centre Christ in the Manger, on the Principle that Corregio has done it in the famous Picture calld the Notte, making all the light proceed from Christ,[1] these tricks of the art, as the[y] may be called, seem to be more properly adapted to Glass painting than any other kind. This middle space will be filled with the Virgin, Christ, Joseph, and Angels, the two smaller spaces on each side I shall fill with the shepherds coming to worship,[2] and the seven divisions below filld with the figures of Faith Hope and Charity and the four Cardinal Virtues, which will make a proper Rustic Base or foundation for the support of the Christian Religion upon the whole it appears to me that chance has presented to us materials so well adapted to our purpose, that if we had the whole window of our own invention and contrivance we should not probably have succeeded better

1 "The head of the Virgin in this capital picture was first a profile. I told him it appeared to me so very *Corregiesque*, that I feared it would be throughout thought too close an imitation of that master. What I then said...had so much weight with him, that when I saw the picture the next time, the head was altered entirely." (Mason's *Anecdotes* in Cotton's *Notes*, 58.) *Cf. post*, p. 111.

2 The two shepherds immediately to the left of the centre are Jervais and Sir Joshua himself. The model for the Virgin and Charity was Mrs Sheridan.

THE WEST WINDOW OF NEW COLLEGE CHAPEL

From Earlom's engraving, 1787

Mr Jervais is happy in the thought of having so large a field for the displ[a]y of his Art and I verily believe it will be the first work of this species of Art, that the world has yet exhibited

I am with the greatest respect
Your most humble
and obedient servant

J REYNOLDS

XLIV[1]

To MRS. HESTER SALUSBURY THRALE

Dear Madam,   London, Sep. 15, 1778.

I would (to use D[r]. Goldsmiths mode) give five pounds to dine with you tomorrow, and I would, as M[r]. Thrale very justly thinks, put off a common dinner engagement, but I have unluckily above a dozen people dine with me tomorrow on Venison which Lord Granby[2] has sent me.

If M[rs]. Montagu has read Evelina, she will to-morrow receive the same satisfaction that we have received in seeing the Author, of which pleasure, anxious as I was, I begun to despair, and little

1 From a facsimile in Tinker's *Dr. Johnson and Fanny Burney*, N.Y. 1911, facing p. 96. The original is in the possession of R. B. Adam, Esq. The recipient (1741–1821), famous bluestocking, was a close friend of Sir Joshua's.

2 *V. ante*, p. 54, n. 3.

expected to find the Author correspond to our romantic imaginations.¹ She seems to be herself the *great sublime she draws*.²

I am, with the greatest respect,
Your most humble
& obedient servant,

JOSHUA REYNOLDS

XLV³

To LORD HARCOURT

My Lord,—   London, Sep. 18, 1778.

I am endeavouring to settle my affairs, working hard and postponing as much business as will enable me to take three more days of pleasure,

1 At the beginning of this year Frances Burney (1752–1840) had published anonymously her first novel, *Evelina*. Both Burke and Reynolds had sat up all night in order to finish it, the latter vowing he would make love to the author if she were a woman. The day before this letter was written Sir Joshua and his two nieces had been the guests of Mrs Thrale at Streatham, where the young author was visiting, and in the course of the day he was let into the secret. Though Mrs Montagu had not read the novel, she was nevertheless properly impressed with its author. (*Diary and Letters of Madame D'Arblay*, ed. Dobson, London, 1904, i, 103 *et seq.*)
2 Altered from Pope's *Essay on Criticism*, iii, 121.
3 From *The Harcourt Papers*, ed. E. W. Harcourt, Oxford, n.d., viii, 270. The recipient was George Simon, second Earl Harcourt (1736–1809), whose portrait was painted by Sir Joshua two years later.

tho' I thought my holydays were over for this summer, but Nuneham is so pleasant both indoors and outdoors that it is irresistible.

My nieces desire their most respectfull compliments, are extremely happy with the thoughts of seeing Nuneham, and extremely proud of the honour of waiting on Lady Harcourt. We propose setting out on Tuesday next, unless I hear to the contrary, and hope to get to Nuneham by dinner time. I mention Tuesday only for the sake of fixing some day; any other would be equaly convenient.

> I am with the greatest respect
> your Lordship's most humble
> and obedient Servant,
>
> JOSHUA REYNOLDS

XLVI[1]

To the Right Reverend ROBERT LOWTH

My Lord   *Leicesterfields Nov. 7th 1778

To the thanks which I took the liberty to transmit to your Lordship for the valuable present which I had the honour so early of receiving;

[1] From the hitherto unpublished original, recently sold by the Messrs Maggs. The recipient (1710–1787) had been elevated to the bishopric of London in the preceding year. From 1741 to 1750 he was Professor of Poetry at Oxford, where he delivered a series of lectures on Hebrew poetry.

I beg leave now to add my further acknowledgments for the pleasure and improvement which
I have receiv'd in its perusal[1]

The easy and intelligible manner in which your
Lordship has condescended to give us the result of
your enquiries into the nature of Hebrew Poetry[2]
has even embolden'd me, ignorant & illiterate to
form a sort of Hypothesis on the subject; but for
which I ought to make many apologies for troubling
your Lordship with it

I am inclined to believe it possible that the
Version of Isaiah such as your Lordship has given
us, may be as much Poetry as the Original
Hebrew; I do not mean that the original is not
Poetry, but that the Translation, preserving the
same equality, proportion, and system of lines, but
above all the same Parellelisms as the original; it
would be Poetry to a Hebrew ear without re-
quiring any other sort of metre

I will venture to risque a question, whether the

1 Lowth had sent him a copy of his translation of *Isaiah*, which
  had just been published. Three days before this letter was
  written, Sir Joshua had sent him a note of thanks, which is still
  extant. *V. post*, Appendix I, under date.
2 Prefixed to the poem there is a "preliminary dissertation" in
  which the author states that though previous writers maintained
  that *Isaiah* was written in prose, it nevertheless had all the
  qualities of Hebrew poetry, "that the Poetical and the Pro-
  phetical character of style and composition, though generally
  supposed to be different, yet are really one and the same".
  (*Op. cit.* London, 1778, p. iii.)

presiding principle of all metre does not consist in repetition; in a certain measure uniformly repeated, or in a repetition of the same sounds, and whether the Hebrew has not the spirit & substance of this rule tho the mode be different.

Repetition of what kind soever it may be is naturally pleasing to me, it makes a stronger impression, and is for that reason much easier retained in the memory, which is one of the peculiar effects of Poetry, and this effect the parelelisms of Hebrew has in common with other Poetry, it, at least has allways had that effect upon me—Isaiah was allways my favorite Book of the old Testament, from having often read it, I had retained a great part of it by heart without any such intention at the time, but rememberd it in the same manner and for the same reason I did Miltons Paradise lost, which I never should have done if either of them had been in Prose.[1]

To shew how much paralelism operates in Sister Arts, it may be observed that Harmony of Colouring, which is in Painting what Metre is in Poetry, is produced entirely by repetition, that is, what ever Colour or Colours are predominant, that same Colour must be often repeated in various parts of the Picture[2]—The beauty of repetition, in

[1] When a boy he seems to have been more impressed with *Ecclesiastes*. (Leslie and Taylor, i, 467.)
[2] "... the same colour which makes the largest mass, [must] be diffused and [must] appear to revive in different parts of the

Architecture, of Pillars and other ornaments
I should imagine proceeds from the same principle
and I believe the result of an enquiry into the
rationale of our passions and affections would be
That similar impulses whether made on the Eye
or the Ear affect us more powerfully than any *one*
impulse, unless that *one* be of a prodigious magnitude indeed such as a view of the Ocean—or God's
commanding the creation of Light.

It really upon the whole appears to me a question, whether if we were early used to this mode or
fashon of Poetry, it would not be thought as
agreable and becoming a dress as Rhime, or any
other kind of metre whether an artfull varied repetition of sound or a repetition of the same measure as in the Greek or Latin Poetry or in our
blank Verse

My Lord

I hesitated a great while whether I should take
the liberty of troubling your Lordship with my
crudities, but the consideration that it would at
least shew your Lordship that I had not immediatly placed the book on its shelve, but had
considerd it with all the attention I was capable,

picture; for a single colour will make a spot or blot." (*Works*,
iii, 156.) In an unpublished MS. in the British Museum (Add.
MSS. 37,053, f. 2) he writes: "I have allways endeavourd in
my Discourses to place the principles of our art parellel with
other arts".

and that I was interested very much in the subject has determined me.

I am with the greatest respect

Your Lordships
most humble
and most obliged servant

JOSHUA REYNOLDS

XLVII[1]

To JOSEPH BANKS

Leicester Fields, Dec. 11th, 1778.

Sir Joshua Reynolds presents his compliments to Mr. Banks and has the pleasure to acquaint him that he was this Evening elected a member of the Club at the Turk's Head, Gerard Street, he need not add unanimously, as one black ball would have excluded him, they hope to have the honour of his Company next Friday.

---

1 From Sotheby's catalogue issued for a sale held June 17, 1899 (p. 70). Joseph Banks (1743–1820), created a baronet in 1781, had succeeded Sir John Pringle as President of the Royal Society only eleven days before this note was written. On October 31 of this year Johnson wrote Langton: "Mr. Banks desires to be admitted; he will be a very honourable accession". (Boswell's *Life*, iii, 365.) He wrote Boswell on November 21: "we talk of electing Banks, the traveller; he will be a reputable member". (*Id.* 368.)

XLVIII[1]

To LORD KEPPEL

Sir,—

London, February 12th, 1779.

Amidst the rejoicing of your friends, I cannot resist offering my congratulations for the complete victory you have gained over your enemies. We talk of nothing but your heroic conduct in voluntarily submitting to suspicions against yourself, in order to screen Sir Hugh Palliser and preserve unanimity in the navy, and the kindness of Sir Hugh in publishing to the world what would otherwise have never been known.

Lord North[2] said of himself, that he was kicked up stairs; I will not use so harsh an expression, but it is the universal opinion that your Court-martial

1 From Keppel's *Life of Augustus Viscount Keppel*, London, 1842, ii, 189 *et seq*. The recipient (1725–1786), Reynolds's host thirty years before on the trip to Minorca, had as leader of the channel fleet decided to attack the French on July 27, 1778. His failure was caused by the disobedience of Sir Hugh Palliser (1723–1796), a Lord of the Admiralty who occupied the third post under him. Although Keppel made no complaint, the truth was soon discovered and the blame placed on Palliser, who first demanded a denial from his superior, and not receiving this, succeeded in having him court-martialed, charging him with misconduct and neglect of duty. This letter was written the day after Keppel's honourable acquittal.

2 Frederick, Lord North (1732–1792), at this time Prime Minister.

is unique of its kind. It would have been thought sufficient if you had had no honour taken from you,—nobody expected that you could have had more heaped on a measure already full.

My opinion in these matters can be of very little value; but it may be some satisfaction to know that this is the opinion of all parties and men of every denomination. Whatever fatigue and expense this business has occasioned is amply repaid you in additional honour and glory; and I hope you begin to think yourself that you have had a bargain.

The illumination yesterday was universal, I believe, without the exception of a single house; we are continuing this night in the same manner.

Poor Sir Hugh's house in Pall Mall was entirely gutted, and its contents burnt in St. James's-square, in spite of a large party of horse and foot, who came to protect it.

Lord North and Lord Bute had their windows broke. The Admiralty gates were unhinged, and the windows of Lord Sandwich and Lord Lisburne broke. Lord Mulgrave's house, I am told, has likewise suffered, as well as Captain Hood's.[1] To-night, I hear, Sir Hugh is to be burnt in effigy before your door.

---

1 Sandwich, Lisburne, and Mulgrave were Lords of the Admiralty. Alexander Hood (1727–1814), later an admiral, and Viscount Bridport, had been in Sir Hugh's division and had given evidence against Keppel.

I have taken the liberty, without waiting for leave, to lend your picture to an engraver,[1] to make a large print from it.

I am, with the greatest respect, your most humble and most obedient servant,

JOSHUA REYNOLDS.

XLIX[2]

To GEORGE MICHAEL MOSER

*Feb 24 [1779.][3]

Sir Joshua Reynolds presents his compliments to M[r] Moser & desires the honor of his company to dinner on Monday next the 1st of March—at 4 o'clock. The favour of an answer is desired.

1 William Doughty (*d.* 1782).
2 From the hitherto unpublished original in my possession. The recipient (1704–1783), a native of Switzerland, was an original member of the Incorporated Society of Artists and a prime mover in the founding of the Royal Academy, of which he was the Keeper. *Cf. ante,* p. 22.
3 Between 1769, when Reynolds was knighted, and 1783, when Moser died, March 1 fell on a Monday twice only, in 1773 and 1779. Under this date in the latter year Sir Joshua noted in his pocket-book that he was "at home" at four.

To LORD OSSORY

My Lord,—   London, Sept. 21, 1779.

I return your Lordship many thanks for the present of venison which I had the honour of receiving to-day, safe, and in perfect good order: it is remarkably fine, and worthy for its beauty to sit for its picture.

I have been as busy this summer in my little way as the rest of the world have been in preparing against the invasion:² from the emptiness of the town I have been able to do more work than I think I ever did in any summer before. My mind has been so much occupied with my business that I have escaped feeling those terrors that seem to have possessed all the rest of mankind. It is to be hoped that it is now all over, at least for this year.

I beg my most respectful compliments to Lady Ossory.³   I am, with the greatest respect,

Your Lordship's most humble
and obedient servant,

JOSHUA REYNOLDS.

1 From Leslie and Taylor, ii, 275. John Fitzpatrick, second Earl of Upper Ossory (1745–1818), whose name frequently appears in the correspondence of George Selwyn, was a close friend and great admirer of Sir Joshua.
2 The French had attacked Jersey in May and had threatened an invasion of England or Ireland throughout the summer.
3 Anne Liddell, the divorced wife of the Duke of Grafton, who had married Ossory in 1769. She was one of Horace Walpole's favourite correspondents.

LI[1]

To NICHOLAS POCOCK

Dear Sir,   Leicester Fields, May 4th, 1780.

Your picture came too late for the exhibition. It is much beyond what I expected from a first essay in oil colours: all the parts separately are extremely well painted; but there wants a harmony in the whole together; there is no union between the clouds, the sea, and the sails. Though the sea appears sometimes as green as you have painted it, yet it is a choice very unfavourable to the art; it seems to me absolutely necessary in order to produce harmony, and that the picture should appear to be painted, as the phrase is, from one palette, that those three great objects of ship-painting should be very much of the same colour as was the practice of Vandevelde, and he seems to be driven to this conduct by necessity.[2] Whatever colour predominates in a picture, that colour must be introduced in other parts; but no green colour, such as you have given to the sea, can make a part of a sky. I believe the truth is, that, however the sea may appear green, when you are looking down on it, and it is very near—at such a distance as

1 From Northcote, ii, 89 *et seq.* The recipient (1751–1821) was one of the original members of the Water Colour Society. His first picture accepted by the Royal Academy was exhibited in 1782.
2 Willem Van De Velde (1633–1707), best known of the Dutch marine-painters. Northcote (ii, 91) disagrees with this remark of Sir Joshua's.

your ships are supposed to be, it assumes the colour of the sky.

I would recommend to you, above all things, to paint from nature instead of drawing; to carry your palette and pencils to the water side. This was the practice of Vernet, whom I knew at Rome;[1] he then shewed me his studies in colours, which struck me very much, for that truth which those works only have which are produced while the impression is warm from nature: at that time he was a perfect master of the character of water, if I may use the expression, he is now reduced to a mere mannerist, and no longer to be recommended for imitation, except you would imitate him by uniting landscape to ship-painting, which certainly makes a more pleasing composition than either alone.

I am, with great respect,

Your most humble and obedient servant,

JOSHUA REYNOLDS.

---

1 When Joseph Vernet (1714–1789) was on his way to Rome, he was so impressed with the storm at sea that he had himself tied to a mast in order to be able to observe it.

LII[1]

To LORD BARRINGTON

Leicester Fields, June 24th. [1780.][2]

My Lord,—

I am sorry that the hurry of business has prevented me from returning the pictures before. I have *endeavoured* to repair Mr. Barrington's[3] in the best manner I can. In regard to the Admiral's[4] picture, I could *scarce* believe it to be the picture I painted, the effect was so completely destroyed by the green sky. This was occasioned by a blunder of my colourman, who sent blue verditer (a colour which changes green within a month), instead of ultramarine, which lasts for ever.[5] However, I

---

1 From Leslie and Taylor, ii, 280 n. William Wildman, second Viscount Barrington (1717–1793), had been painted by Reynolds in 1762.

2 Graves and Cronin (56) in reprinting the letter assign it to 1779. Inasmuch as the admiral's portrait was not begun until November 18 in that year, the earliest possible date would be 1780.

3 The recipient's brother, the Hon. Shute Barrington (1734–1826), who sat (as "Mr. Barrington") in December, 1757, February, 1759, and January, 1762.

4 The Hon. Samuel Barrington (1729–1800), Admiral of the White.

5 "Sir Joshua once bought, at a very considerable price, of some itinerant foreigner, I believe a German, a parcel of what he pretended was genuine ultramarine, which, in point of color, seemed fully to answer its title. Without bringing it to any chemical test, the artist ventured to use it, and by it spoiled, as

74

have made such a background now as I think best
corresponds with the head, and sets it off to the
best advantage.

I am, with the greatest respect,
your most humble and most obedient servant,

JOSHUA REYNOLDS.

LIII[1]

To SAMUEL JOHNSON

Dear Sir　　　　　　　　[December 23, 1780.]

I have receivd the enclosd from Miss
Monckton[2] I have answerd it that I am myself
engaged as I really am to Mrs Walsingham[3] what
answer do you give I shall meet you on Thursday

he assured me, several pictures; for the fictitious pigment soon
changed into a muddy green, which he was obliged to repair,
by painting over it." (Mason's *Anecdotes* in Cotton's *Notes*, 54.)
"Sir Joshua was ever careful about procuring unadulterated
articles of every sort, and has often desired me to inform the
colour-man, that he should not regard any price that might be
demanded, provided the colours were genuine." (Northcote,
ii, 22.)

1 From a facsimile in R. B. Adam's *Catalogue of the Johnsonian
Collection*, Buffalo, 1921, under "Reynolds".
2 Mary Monckton, later Countess of Cork and Orrery (1746–
1840), the bluestocking whose "vivacity enchanted the Sage".
3 Charlotte Williams Walsingham (*d.* 1790), whose husband, the
Hon. Robert Boyle Walsingham, had gone down with his ship,
Thunderer, in October, 1779.

at Lady Lucans¹ or if you will give me leave to
send my coach for you, we will go together

I have a sitter waiting so you must excuse the
blots
                                                    Your

                                                    J R

                                    LIV²

                        To WILLIAM JOHNSON

                                    January 17th, 1781.

   ...I sincerely rejoice at your success and whatever is in my power to promote it you may always
command; I am now drawing a whole length of
Mr. Barwell, and his son, for Mr. Hastings,³ when
the picture goes to India, I shall write at the same

1 Margaret Smyth Bingham, Countess of Lucan (*d.* 1814), an
amateur painter who receives extraordinary praise in Horace
Walpole's letters. Few of the numerous engagements with her
which Sir Joshua has recorded in his existing pocket-books took
place on a Thursday. The one here referred to is most probably
that of December 29, 1780, since he was the guest of Mrs
Walsingham on the previous Friday, December 23.
2 From Cotton's *Gleanings*, 154. In November, 1913, the original
was in the possession of Walter R. Benjamin, Esq., of New York.
(*The Collector*, xxvii, i, 2.) The recipient (*d.* 1799), Sir Joshua's
nephew, had arrived in India in 1774 and was clerk of the
Crown in Calcutta. (Debrett's *East India Kalendar*...*for*...1791,
70.)
3 Warren Hastings (1732–1818), famous Governor-General of
India. Richard Barwell (*d.* 1804) had returned from India in
the previous year. He and his son began sitting for the portrait
in the middle of October.

time in your favour. Mr. Macpherson,[1] who is appointed one of the Supreme Council, has promised me in a very emphatic manner, to serve you in whatever you may want his assistance. I have given him your name in writing, and you will of course wait upon him, as soon as he arrives. . . .

Let me recommend you to make yourself master of the politicks of India of every kind,—with superior knowledge, things fall into your hands, and but little interest is required. I would advise you to learn, at your leisure hours, the Persian language, which would certainly facilitate your progress, and contribute to make you a useful man. To make it people's *interest* to advance you, that their business will be better done by you than by any other person, is the only solid foundation of success; the rest is accident.

I am, your most affectionate Uncle,

JOSHUA REYNOLDS.

My compliments to Sir Robert and Lady Chambers.[2]

1 John Macpherson (1744–1821), who succeeded Hastings as Governor-General in 1785 and was created baronet the following year.
2 Sir Robert Chambers (1737–1803), an original member of the Club, had been appointed judge in 1773, when Sir Joshua had painted his portrait for the Thrales.

77

LV[1]

To MRS. THEOPHILA PALMER GWATKIN

My dear Offy,   *January 30th, 1781.

I intended to have answered your letter immediately, and to have wrote at the same time to Mr. Gwatkin,[2] but was prevented, and have been prevented every evening since. However, I proposed doing so this evening, and disengaged myself from Mrs. Elliot's (where Polly[3] is gone) on purpose. But this moment Mr. Edmund Burke has called on me, and proposes a party, but desires I would write while he waits at my elbow, for that he will add something himself. You must suppose, therefore, that I have wished and expressed everything that affection to you and friendship to Mr. Gwatkin would dictate.

That you may be as happy as you both deserve is my wish, and you will be the happiest couple in England. So God bless you. I will leave the rest to Mr. Burke.[4]

Your most affectionate Uncle,

J. REYNOLDS.

1 From Leslie and Taylor, ii, 318. The original is in the possession of R. G. Gwatkin, Esq.
2 Robert Lovell Gwatkin, who had just married the recipient.
3 Mary Palmer, sister of the bride (*cf. ante*, Letter xxxix). I assume that "Mrs. Elliot" was the wife of Edward Eliot, Knight of the Shire for Cornwall, whose name frequently appears in Sir Joshua's pocket-books.
4 Leslie and Taylor add Burke's continuation of the letter.

LVI[1]

To FRANCES REYNOLDS

Dear Sister   [1781.][2]

I am very much obliged to you for your kind
and generous offer in regard to the house at Richmond[3] not only in giving me leave to use it
occasionally but even as long as I live provided
I will give it to you, but as I have no such thoughts
at present I can only thank you for your kindness
—tho I am much older than you[4] I hope I am
not yet arrived to dotage as you seem to think
I am, voluntarily to put myself in the situation of

1 From the original in the possession of Rupert Colomb, Esq.,
  now lent to the Royal Academy. First published in Hill's
  Johnsonian Miscellanies, Oxford, 1897, ii, 456 *et seq*. The recipient
  (1729–1808), Johnson's "Renny dear", was Sir Joshua's sister,
  who had kept house for him when he settled in London after his
  Italian trip. They had quarrelled, and she was living at the
  home of John Hoole, translator of Ariosto. One of three letters
  to her from Dr Johnson may refer to this request of hers for the
  house at Richmond. (*Letters of Samuel Johnson*, ed. Hill, ii, 84,
  397; *Johnsonian Miscellanies*, ed. Hill, ii, 455.)
2 The letter is endorsed by Fanny: "Sir Joshua—I believe in '81".
3 "Of the small villa…which Sir Joshua built for his recreation,
  on Richmond Hill, Sir William Chambers was the architect;
  but not because it was intended to make any display of taste in
  the building, for convenience alone was consulted in it. In the
  summer season it was the frequent custom of Sir Joshua to dine
  at this place with select parties of his friends." (Northcote, i,
  304.)
4 He was six years her senior.

79

receiving the favour of living in my own house instead of conferring the favour of letting you live in it[1]

I am your most affectionate

Brother

J REYNOLDS

I have enclosed a Bank Bill of ten Pounds[2]

LVII[3]

To EDMUND BURKE

Dear Sir,   Brussels, August 2nd, 1781.

We arrived at Brussels the thirtieth, and shall probably set out this evening for Antwerp.[4] Nothing hitherto has happened worth mentioning, nor have we seen any pictures better than we have

1 On his death the house became the property of his niece, Mary Palmer, who had earlier described it as "a house stuck upon the top of a hill, without a bit of garden or ground of any sort near it but what is as public as St. James's Park". (Leslie and Taylor, ii, 542.)

2 In a MS. seen by Taylor Frances mentions "the income allowed her by her brother, as sufficient to keep her within the sphere of gentility, 'without pecuniary schemes to raise it higher'". (Leslie and Taylor, i, 92 n.)

3 From Cotton's *Gleanings*, 159 *et seq.* The letter is addressed to Edmund Burke, Esq., Charles Street, St. James's Square.

4 Accompanied by his friend Philip Metcalfe, Sir Joshua had left London for the continent on July 24. (Leslie and Taylor, ii, 329.) The extensive notes which he made on the pictures seen were first printed by Malone (*Works*, ii, 245 *et seq.*) and are now in the British Museum.

at home. Ghent and Alost have two or three
pictures of Rubens, and Brussels perhaps a dozen,
the people seem to make so much of his works that
it requires some circumspection not to run on the
other side; the pictures hitherto have not answered
our expectation. We have been very well amused,
and pass out time very agreeably. Yesterday we
dined at Mr. Fitzherbert's with the Duke of Richmond, and Mr. Lenox, and we all behaved very
well.[1] I don't know whether I might not expect
too much, but I thought Mr. Fitz. would have laid
himself [out] more for our amusement, he has returned our visit, and given us a dinner, or rather,
let us dine with him, at the same time with the
Duke of Richmond, and that's all.

The Emperor will probably not return to
Brussels, he has left an impression on every rank of
people very much to his honor.[2]

The Duchess of Chandos recommended to him
in a very absurd manner the Princess Royal for a
wife. The Emperor said he was too old for her, but
she would not accept the excuse, and added that
her Duke was as much older than she was, and yet

1 Alleyne Fitzherbert, later Baron St Helens (1753–1839), was at
this time minister at Brussels. Charles Lennox, third Duke of
Richmond (1734/5–1806), had succeeded his father in 1750.
Perhaps "Mr. Lenox" was his nephew, Charles Lennox, later
fourth Duke of Richmond (1764–1819).
2 Joseph II had visited Brussels from the end of May until the
second week in July.

they lived very happily together,[1] Mr. Fitzherbert said the Emperor told this to every person he saw that day. We propose going to Dusseldorf, consequently shall take the Spa in our way.

I write with continual interruption, having so little to say, and so little time to say that little, that I believe I should not have ventured to have wrote, if I had not had an opportunity of inclosing my letter in a cover to Mr. Frazer.[2]

The chaise is at the door for Antwerp, where if anything occurs you will hear from me again. We shall stay there, as we do at every other place, just as long as we can amuse ourselves, and hitherto we have been exactly of the same opinion.

Yours,[3]

JOSHUA REYNOLDS.

1 In 1777 the Duke of Chandos had married Anne Eliza, widow of Roger Hope Elletson. The Emperor was at this time forty years old and the Princess Royal, Charlotte Augusta Matilda, fifteen. In 1797 she married the King of Würtemburg.
2 I infer that this was one W. Fraser, Under-Secretary of State. *Cf.* the *Royal Kalendar...for...*1781, 110.
3 The conclusion is so printed in Leslie and Taylor (ii, 646). Cotton states that it has been torn off.

LVIII[1]

To EDMUND BURKE

Hague, August 14, 1781.

We have been here three days, and propose staying here three days longer, to enjoy ourselves after our fatigue. I promise you we have not been idle. Hitherto, every minute of the day has been employed in travelling or staring. The Prince of Orange's gallery is the only magazine of pictures that we have seen here, and the only we are likely to see. The possessor of another collection, Mr. Van Uteren,[2] is not in town, he is at Amsterdam. The Greffier[3] has sent to him, but it is suspected it will be without effect, as he has the keys with him, and will never suffer his pictures to be seen but when he his present. The Greffier has shown us every civility possible; he returned our visit immediately, and we dined with him the next day. He is a most amiable character, of the greatest simplicity of manners, and has not the least tincture of that insolence of office, or, I should say, (thinking of a person at Brussels,) that indolence of office, of those who think their whole business is to appear negligent and at their ease. By the attention which

1 From the *Correspondence of...Burke*, London, 1844, ii, 424 *et seq.*
2 *V. post*, p. 84, n. 3.
3 Henry Fagel (1707–1790), whose collection of pictures is mentioned in Sir Joshua's Journal. (*Works*, ii, 351.) An account of his life appears in the *London Chronicle* for October 23–26, 1790 (lxviii, 408).

6-2

has been paid us by the Greffier, his nephew, and
the rest of his family, the attention of the town upon
us has been much excited. This is but a small place,
and in many respects like Bath, where the people
have nothing to do but to talk of each other; and
it may be compared to Bath, likewise, for its
beauty. It abounds in squares which you would
be charmed with, as they are full of trees; not disposed in a meagre, scanty row, but are more like
woods with walks in the middle.

The Prince of Orange,[1] whom we saw two or
three times, is very like King George, but not so
handsome. He has a heavy look, short person,
with somewhat a round belly.[2] The Greffier frequently expressed his concern that he was not able
to do for us all he wished, such as introducing us
to the prince, &c., on account of the situation of
affairs. We have seen the collection I mentioned
in the beginning, which was scarce worth the
trouble of sending so far for the keys.[3] Dutch
pictures are a representation of nature, just as it is
seen in a camera-obscura. After having seen the

1 William V, father of the first king of Holland, William I. Sir
  Joshua had seen him two days before this at "the Review".
  (Leslie and Taylor, ii, 331.)
2 *Cf.* Falstaff's description of himself (*Henry IV, Part II*, 1, ii, 212).
3 In his notes on the pictures at the Hague (*Works*, ii, 343 *et seq.*)
  he refers only to the two collections of the Prince of Orange,
  and to those of Greffier Fagel and M. Van Hecheren. I therefore infer that the Van Uteren in the opening paragraph was
  the same individual as the Van Hecheren in the Journal.

best of each master, one has no violent desire of
seeing any more. They are certainly to be admired,
but do not shine much in description. A figure
asleep, with another figure tickling his or her nose,
which is a common subject with the painters of
this school, however admirable their effect, would
have no effect in writing.

Amsterdam, August 24.

The above letter was written, as you see, at
the Hague; to-morrow we leave Amsterdam for
Dusseldorp. The face of this country is very
striking from its being unlike every thing else. The
length and straightness of their artificial roads,
often with double rows of trees, which, in the perspective, finish in a point;—the perseverance of
their industry and labour to form those dykes,
and preserve them in such perfect repair, is an idea
that must occur to every mind, and is truly sublime. This country is, I should imagine, the most
artificial country in the world. This city is more
like Venice than any other place I ever saw. In
many places, it is an exact likeness, where the
water reaches to the houses; but this is not common. In the middle of every street are canals; and
on each side those canals, quays and rows of trees.
Another idea of their industry and perseverance,
which amounts, I think, to the sublime, is, that the
foundation of their buildings, which is piles, costs
as much as what appears above ground, both in

labour and expense. The Stadthouse is founded on 13,659 piles. I have often thought the habit they have acquired of fighting against nature, has given them a disposition never to leave nature as they find her. But in order to see the Dutch taste in its highest degree, we spent a day in North Holland. We went to a village called Brock, which appeared so different from any thing we had seen before, that it appeared rather like an enchanted village, such as we read of in the Arabian tales;[1]— not a person to be seen, except a servant here and there. The houses are very low, with a door towards the street, which is not used, and never has been used, except when they go out of it to be married, after which it is again shut up. The streets, if they may be so called, for carriages cannot enter them, are sanded with fine ink-sand; the houses painted from top to bottom, green, red, and all sorts of colours. The little gardens, with little fountains and flower-knots, as neat as possible; and trees cut into all kinds of shapes. Indeed, I much doubt if you can find a tree in its natural shape all over Holland, and we may add, nor water neither, which is everywhere kept within bounds. We have been extraordinarily well received by Mr. Hope;[2]

[1] Sir Joshua's copy of *The Arabian Nights* is in the possession of the Brick Row Book Shop, New York.

[2] Henry Hope (*d*. 1811) of the banking-house of Hope and Co., Amsterdam. *V. Dict. Nat. Biog.* under "John Williams Hope". His pictures are described in Sir Joshua's Journal. (*Works*, ii, 358 *et seq.*)

we are every day dining or supping with him, and one great dinner seemed to be made on purpose for us.

Dusseldorp, August 30, 1781.

On the 25th we set out from Amsterdam, and to-morrow we propose going from hence to Aix-la-Chapelle; and then, after staying a day or two there, turn our faces directly for England. If I do not send away this letter now, I shall bring it with me to England. I really did intend writing to you from the Hague and from Amsterdam; but the difficulty of finding time to finish my letter, has been the reason of my carrying it about with me

We are very well contented with our visit to Dusseldorp. Rubens reigns here and revels. His pictures of the Fallen Angels, and the Last Judgment, give a higher idea of his genius than any other of his works.[1] There is one picture of Raffaelle in his first manner, which is the only picture of consequence of the Roman school.[2] The collection is made up of Flemish and Dutch pictures, but they are the best of those schools. The ease with which this gallery is seen, and the indulgence to the young painters who wish to copy any of the pictures, is beyond any thing I ever saw in any other place. We have had every attention possible from the keeper of the pictures, who, as soon as he knew who I was, sent into the country to his

1 *Cf. Works*, ii, 398 *et seq.*
2 *Cf. Works*, ii, 384.

principal,[1] who is likewise president of the academy, who immediately came to town, and has been attending us ever since.

Yours sincerely,

J. REYNOLDS.

LIX[2]

To OZIAS HUMPHRY

*February 1st. [1782.][3]

Sir Joshua Reynolds' compliments to Mr. Humphry, he has been informed by Bartolozzi[4] that Mr. Humphry had sent to him for the Lord Chancellor's picture, begs he will be so kind as to inform Sir Joshua whether he has any such order from the Lord Chancellor,[5] or, upon what authority he sent for it.

1 Lambert Kraye. *Cf.* Leslie and Taylor, ii, 333.
2 From Williamson's *Life and Works of Ozias Humphry*, London, 1918, 101. The recipient (1743–1810), miniature-painter, had settled in London in 1764 at Reynolds's suggestion. *Cf. ante*, Letter VIII.
3 According to Algernon Graves (Williamson, *ibid.*), this letter belongs to the period of 1780 or 1781. I have dated it 1782, because in that year Bartolozzi engraved Thurlow's portrait.
4 Francesco Bartolozzi (1727–1815), famous engraver.
5 Edward Thurlow, Lord Thurlow (1735–1806), Lord Chancellor from 1778 to 1783, who was sitting for his portrait in October, 1781.

LXI

To THOMAS COLLINGWOOD

Sir

Leicesterfields Feb 28th 1782

I beg my most respectfull Compts. may be presented to the Governors, I consider the nomination of myself to be one of the Stewards as a great honour conferr'd on me and will certainly attend at the Hospital on the Anniversary in May next.[2]

I am with great respect
Sir
Your most obedient
humble servant
J REYNOLDS

1 From a photostat of the original in the Foundling Hospital. First published in Brownlow's *Memoranda; or Chronicles of the Foundling Hospital*, London, 1847, 89 n. The recipient was secretary of the Hospital from 1758 to 1790.

2 In the pocket-book for this year under May 8 is the following note: "Foundling to see Pictures". The governors met each year on the second Wednesday in May. Unpublished records of the Hospital reveal that on December 26, 1759, "Mr. Joshua Reynolds of Newport Street, having presented to this Corporation a fine portrait of the Earl of Dartmouth", had been unanimously elected a "Governor and Guardian of the hospital".

LXI[1]

To JAMES BEATTIE

London, March 31st, 1782.

...I am very much flattered by your giving me a sight of your Essay,[2] which I assure you I have read over and over with the greatest attention, and, I may add, with the greatest pleasure and improvement. About twenty years since I thought much on this subject,[3] and am now glad to find many of those ideas which then passed in my mind put in such good order by so excellent a metaphysician. My view of the question did not extend beyond my own profession; it regarded only the beauty of form which I attributed entirely to custom or habit. You have taken a larger compass, including, indeed, everything that gives delight, every mental and corporeal excellence, and have adorned your philosophy with the most happy illustrations, which are both convincing and entertaining. Indeed, the question appears to me to be very thoroughly investigated. I thought once I should have returned you an Essay as long as

1 From Margaret Forbes's *Beattie and His Friends*, Westminster, 1904, 179 *et seq.*
2 Beattie had sent him in MS. the essay on Beauty in his *Dissertation on Imagination*, which was published the following year in his *Dissertations Moral and Critical* (pp. 110–142).
3 *V. post*, p. 93, n. 1.

yours. I wrote many sheets and some long reasoning, but found them at last entirely needless, that you had done all that was necessary, and in a much better manner, so threw them in the fire.

I am much obliged to you for the honourable place you have given me cheek by jowl with Raphael and Titian, but I seriously think these names are too great to be associated with any modern name whatever; even if that modern was equal to either of them it would oppose too strongly our prejudices. I am far from wishing to decline the honour of having my name inserted, but I should think it will do better by itself—supposing it were thus: "but we do not find this affectation in the pictures of Reynolds, and in his discourses he has particularly cautioned the student against it";[1] and in the second place where I am mentioned, leaving out Titian, I shall make a respectable figure.[2] Sometimes by endeavouring to do too much the effect of the whole is lost. I fear you will think me very impertinent in taking such liberties.

Your idea of producing the line of beauty by taking the medium of the two extremes, exactly

1 Adopted without a verbal change. *Cf. Dissertation*, 123.
2 "Andromache smiling in tears would be as interesting an object now, as she was three thousand years ago: and the Venus, and the Lavinia, of the Mantuan poet, if copied by Reynolds, would still be the perfection of feminine grace, and feminine tenderness." (*Dissertation*, 138.)

coincides with my idea, and its beauty I think may fairly be deduced from habit. All lines are either curved or straight, and that which partakes equally of each is the medium or average of all lines and therefore more beautiful than any other line; notwithstanding this, an artist would act preposterously that should take every opportunity to introduce this line in his works as Hogarth himself did, who appears to have taken an aversion to a straight line. His pictures therefore want that line of firmness and stability which is produced by straight lines;[1] this conduct therefore may truly be said to be unnatural, for it is not the conduct of Nature.

What you have imputed to convenience and contrivance, I think may without violence be put to the account of habit, as we are more used to that form in nature (and I believe in art, too) which is the *most* convenient. Fitness and beauty being always united in animals, as well as men, they are fit in proportion as they are beautiful, and beautiful in proportion as they are fit, which makes it difficult to determine what is the original cause; as I said before, I am inclined to habit, and that we determine by habit in regard to beauty without waiting for the slower determination of reason. I am aware that this reasoning goes upon a supposition that we are more used to beauty than

1 Beattie adopted this suggestion, retaining Sir Joshua's phrase. *Cf. Dissertation*, 119.

deformity, and that we are so, I think, I have proved in a little Essay which I wrote about twenty-five years since, and which Dr. Johnson published in his *Idler*, if you think it worth while to look into it.[1]

May not all beauty proceeding from association of ideas be reduced to the principle of habit or experience? You see I am bringing everything into my old principle, but I will now have done, for fear I should throw this letter likewise in the fire; and now conclude with my sincere thanks for the pleasure you have given and indeed the compliment you have paid me in thinking me worthy of seeing this work in manuscript. I ought likewise to make some apology for keeping it so long. The truth is, when I received it I was very busy in writing notes on Mason's translation of Fresnoy's poem on painting, which Mr. Mason waited for, and it is now printing at York.[2] . . .

1 *Idler*, no. 82, published Nov. 10, 1759. Beattie quotes from it in his *Dissertation* (120 n.).
2 *V. post*, p. 100, n. 3.

LXII[1]

To THOMAS WARTON

Dear Sir   London May 13th 1782

This is the first minute I have had to thank you for the Verses which I had the honour and pleasure of receiving a week ago.[2] It is a bijoux, it is a beautifull little thing, and I think I should have equally admired it, if I had not been so much interested in it as I certainly am; I owe you great obligations for the Sacrifice which you have made, or pretend to have made, to modern Art, I say pretend, for tho' it it allowed that you have like a true Poet feigned marvellously well, and have opposed the two different stiles with the skill of a Connoiseur, yet I may be allowed to entertain some doubts of the sincerity of your conversion, I have no great confidence in the recantation of such an old offender.[3]

It is short, but it is a complete composition; it is a whole, the struggle is I think eminently beautifull—

From bliss long felt unwillingly we part
Ah spare the weakness of a lovers heart!

1 From the original in the British Museum (Add. MSS. 36,526 D). First published in Mant's *Poetical Works of Thomas Warton*, Oxford, 1802, i, p. lxxx. The recipient (1728–1790), historian of English poetry, became poet-laureate in 1785, partly through Sir Joshua's efforts. (Leslie and Taylor, ii, 471.)
2 Warton had sent him his *Verses on Sir Joshua Reynolds's Painted Window at New-College Oxford*, which had just been published.
3 Alluding, of course, to Warton's classical tendencies.

94

It is not much to say that your Verses are by far the best that ever my name was concernd in. I am sorry therefore my name was not hitchd in in the body of the Poem, if the title page should be lost it will appear to be addressd to Mr Jervais[1]

> I am Dear Sir
> with the greatest respect
>> your most humble
>> and obliged servant
>>> J REYNOLDS.

LXIII[2]

To ——

June 6, 1782.

...I shall certainly execute the commission which his Grace[3] has ordered, with the greatest care possible, as soon as ever I receive the picture, and hope it will be such a picture as will give an opportunity of doing something that shall correspond to his Grace's idea. I knew very little of

1 Sir Joshua's name also appears on the first page of the poem. However, in the second edition, which came out the following year, "Reynolds" is substituted for "Artist" in the conclusion.
2 From *Rutland*, iv, 244. I am indebted to my friend, L. Bradner, Esq., of Brown University, for calling my attention to this letter.
3 Charles Manners, fourth Duke of Rutland (1754–1787), who had succeeded to the dukedom in 1779.

Lord Robert,¹ but was very well acquainted with
his Grace's great affection to him. I therefore felt
and sympathised with him. I really think in losing
him we have paid the full value of what we have
got; it is the general opinion that we have lost the
most promising youth in the whole navy, and I am
sure from what I saw of him and the letters I have
seen from him, I am most perfectly inclined to
confirm their opinion. I beg my most respectful
compliments to their Graces....

LXIV²

To the DUKE OF RUTLAND

London, September 13, 1782.

...As the fifteenth is so near, when your
Grace said you should be in town, I have nothing
to say but what may be deferred till that time. The
business of this letter is to thank your Grace—
which I forgot to do when I was at Chevely³—for
the letter, which I received from the keeper of the

1 Lord Robert Manners (1758–1782), captain, R.N., and brother
of the above. He had died from wounds received while serving
under Rodney in the West Indies. Sir Joshua was commissioned
to paint a posthumous portrait of him.
2 From *Rutland*, iii, 61.
3 Cheveley Park, near Newmarket, one of the principal seats
of the Dukes of Rutland, which Sir Joshua had visited during
the last week in August.

park, to inform me that a buck was ready whenever I should send for it, and I am now ready for
the buck. I have company dine with me next
Thursday, which I think is the nineteenth, and
should be glad to have it by that time.¹ I should
have wrote to the keeper not to trouble your Grace,
but I have forgot his name, though I have not
forgot his countenance, which struck me very
much. . . .

LXV²

To WILLIAM JOHNSON

My Dear Nephew   London Jan 19 1783

I intended to have taken this opportunity of
paying the debt I owe you of a long Letter, but
delayed it on account of a violent inflammation in
my Eyes which prevented me from writing.³ I am
not yet recover'd, but Mr Meyers⁴ sets out to-
morrow morning which must apologise for the
shortness of this letter, the whole business of which

1 Pocket-book, September 19: "Mr. Gibbon, &c."
2 From the hitherto unpublished original in the possession of the
  Brick Row Book Shop, New York.
3 Late in the previous year he had suffered from a "slight
  paralytick affection". (*Works*, i, p. cvi.)
4 George Charles Meyer, who became Assistant Secretary to the
  Preparer of Reports in the Revenue Department at Calcutta.
  (*Bengal Calendar for 1788*, 12.) He was the son of Jeremiah
  Meyer (1735?–1789), miniature-painter.

is to recommend and introduce Mr Meyers to you. He is the son of a particular friend of mine, and I have no doubt you will do him, on my account, as well as his own, whatever services are in your power; your character is such that I dont wonder every Father wishes to have his son introduced to you. I suppose you have heard that Offe is married to Mr Gwatkin and has got a daughter.[1]

I beg my Love to your Brother—my Neeces & Mr Young.[2] To Governour Hastings Sir Robert Chambers & Lady Chambers & Mr Macpherson.[3]

I remain

Yours most affectionately

JOSHUA REYNOLDS

Polly desires her love
to you and all her
cousins

---

1 *Cf. post*, p. 105, n. 2.
2 Richard Johnson was Accomptant General to the Revenue Department; his two sisters in India were Elizabeth and Jane. "Mr Young" was Philip Yonge, frequently mentioned in Mary Palmer's letters.
3 *Cf. ante*, Letter LIV.

LXVI[1]

To the Right Reverend THOMAS PERCY

My Lord,   London, Feb. 12, 1783.

I am ashamed of not answering your Lordship's letter sooner, but I will not fill this with apologies. I spoke to Sir Joseph Banks about it, who says, that on the receipt of Mr. Trocke's letter he gave the bill of lading, which he received from Mr. Trocke, to his broker; that, on his leaving town, at the end of August, he had not received from his broker any account of the wine being arrived; that during his stay in the country, he having confidence in his broker and his broker in him, nothing passed between them concerning the wine; that Mr. Trocke's letter of September 30 was answered, not by return of the post, as Sir Joseph thought it useless, but with his first leisure. On his return to town he found the wine lodged in Mr. Colman's[2] cellar, according to his orders, and forwarded, without delay, the certificate to Mr. Trocke.

The wine was tasted, at the Turk's Head, the meeting before the last, and was pronounced to be

1 From Nichols's *Illustrations of...Literary History*, London, 1858, viii, 205. Percy had sent the Club a hogshead of claret and, not hearing of its arrival, had written to Sir Joshua. *V.* Gaussen's *Percy: Prelate and Poet*, London, 1908, 194.

2 George Colman, the elder (1732–1794), dramatist, who had been elected to the Club in 1773.

good wine, but not yet fit for drinking; we have, therefore, postponed any further progress in it till next year, when, I hope, your Lordship will have an opportunity of tasting it yourself.

I wished to have an opportunity of sending you my last Discourse,[1] though it is scarce worth sending so many miles.

The Club seems to flourish this year; we have had Mr. Fox, Burke, and Johnson very often. I mention those because they are, or have been, the greatest truants.[2] Mr. Mason has at last published his translation of Fresnoy,[3] which I would send your Lordship, with the Discourse, if I knew how.

I beg my most respectful compliments to Mrs. Percy, and am, with the greatest respect,

Your Lordship's most humble and most obedient servant,

JOSHUA REYNOLDS.

1 The eleventh, which had been delivered at the Royal Academy December 10, 1782.
2 The Club's records show that Johnson and Fox attended none of the dinners in 1781 and that in 1782 Johnson and Burke were present three times and Fox once only. In each of these years the Club met sixteen times. *V. Annals of the Club*, London, 1914, 26 *et seq.*
3 *The Art of Painting of Charles Alphonse Du Fresnoy. Translated into English Verse by William Mason, M.A. With Annotations by Sir Joshua Reynolds, Knt. President of the Royal Academy*, York, 1783. It was reviewed in the *Gentleman's Magazine* for this month (liii, 159).

LXVII[1]

To the Reverend GEORGE CRABBE

Dear Sir,   [March 4, 1783.]

I have returned your poem with Dr. Johnson's letter[2] to me—if you knew how sparing Dr. Johnson deals out his praises, you would be very well content with what he says.[3] I feel myself in some measure flattered in the success of my prognostication.

Yours sincerely...

LXVIII[4]

To LORD HARDWICKE

My Lord   March 5 1783

The subject which your Lordship mentions of the interview between the Duke of Monmouth and James the 2ᵈ[5] is certainly better calculated for a

---

1 From Huchon's *Crabbe*, Paris, 1906, 187 n. The recipient (1754–1832), clergyman and poet, had been introduced to Sir Joshua by Burke in 1781.

2 *V. Letters of Johnson*, ed. Hill, ii, 287. The poem discussed was *The Village*, which was published on May 23.

3 "I am very unwilling", said Johnson to Boswell, "to read the manuscripts of authours, and give them my opinion." (Boswell's *Life*, ii, 195.) Some of Johnson's changes in the poem are given by Boswell. (*Id.* iv, 175, n. 4.)

4 From the hitherto unpublished original in the British Museum (Add. MSS. 35,350, f. 48). For the recipient *v. ante*, Letter XXIII.

5 When the Duke of Monmouth (1649–1685) had been captured after his unsuccessful revolt, he "fell upon his knees, and begged his life in the most abject terms. He even signed a paper,

Picture, than that of the old Duke of Bedford, tho
I think even this has scarce enough of intelligible
action and perhaps the expression is too delicate
for our art. But the insuperable objection to subjects of that period, is the dress. The first effect of
such a picture will be allways mean and vulgar
and to depart from the Costume is as bad on the
other side[1] It was the late Charles Townsend that
recommended to me the interview of The Duke of
Bedford and K. James as a subject for a Picture.[2]

I wish it was in my power to answer the Post-
script in regard to a subject for the accession of the
present R Family What Your Lordship cannot
find is very unlikely to occur to me

I am with the greatest respect

Your Lordships most humb[l]e
and obedient servan[t,]

J REYNOLD[S.]

offered him by the king, declaring his own illegitimacy; and
then the stern tyrant assured him, that his crime was of such a
nature, as could not be pardoned. The duke perceiving that he
had nothing to hope from the clemency of his uncle, recollected
his spirits, rose up, and retired with an air of disdain". (Goldsmith's *History of England*, iv, London, 1771, 9 *et seq.*)

1 Sir Joshua had vainly urged West to clothe the characters in his
"Death of Wolfe" in the costumes of antiquity, but later admitted that he had erred. *Cf. Works*, ii, 36.

2 Charles Townshend (1725–1767), Chancellor of the Exchequer,
had sat to Sir Joshua for his portrait in 1755 and 1764. The
subject he suggested was the interview in which the distracted
king, asking Bedford for aid, is reminded that William Russell
(Bedford's son) had been executed as a rebel.

LXIX[1]

To VALENTINE GREEN

[May 6, 1783.]

Sir Joshua Reynolds presents his compliments to Mr. Green—if the choice of the engraver depends on him, he will certainly remember Mr. Green's first application. Her wish, and the ladies who were with her when she sat, appears to be for an engraved print, not a mezzotinto; but the picture is but just began, and in a state of uncertainty whether it will be a picture worth making a print from it or not.

LXX[2]

To VALENTINE GREEN

Sir,—   Leicester-fields, June 1, 1783.

You have the pleasure, if it is any pleasure to you, of reducing me to a most mortifying situa-

1 From *The Literary Gazette*, 1822, 85. The recipient (1739–1813), distinguished mezzotinter, had just applied for permission to engrave the portrait of Mrs Siddons as "The Tragic Muse".

2 From *The Literary Gazette*, 1822, 86. This and the preceding reference were kindly supplied by Mr W. T. Whitley. The letter is addressed "To Valentine Green, Esq. Associate of the Royal Academy, Mezzotinto Engraver to his Majesty, and to the Elector Palatine". A rough draft of it, published by Leslie and Taylor, ii, 425 *et seq.*, is in the possession of Rupert Colomb, Esq., and is now lent to the Royal Academy. It is in answer to an indignant letter from Green (*v. post*, Appendix III, Letter F). Mrs Siddons's note, in which she desires the engraving to be done by Francis Haward, is published in Whitley's *Artists and their Friends in England*, ii, 10.

tion: I must either treat your hard accusations of being a liar, with the contempt of silence (which you and your friends may think implies guilt) or I must submit to vindicate myself, like a criminal, from this heavy charge. I mentioned in conversation, when I had the honour of seeing you last at my house, that Mrs. Siddons had wrote a note to me respecting the print. When I assert any thing, I have the happiness of knowing that my friends believe what I say, without being put to the blush, as I am at present, by being forced to produce proofs, since you tell me in your letter, *that Mrs. Siddons never did write or even speak to me in favour of any other artist.*

But supposing Mrs. Siddons out of the question, my words (on which you grounded your *demand as right, and not as a favour*) I do not see can any way be interposed as such an absolute promise; I intended it to mean only, that you having made the first application, should be remembered by me, and that it should turn the scale in your favour, supposing equality in other respects. You say you wait the result of my determination; what determination can you expect after such a letter?

You have been so good as to recommend to me *to give for the future unequivocal answers.* I shall immediately follow your advice, and do now in the most unequivocal manner inform you, that you shall NOT do the print.

MRS SIDDONS AS THE TRAGIC MUSE

From Haward's engraving, 1787

I am, Sir, with all humility, and due acknow-
ledgment of your dignity,

Your most humble Servant,

JOSHUA REYNOLDS.

LXXI[1]

To MRS. THEOPHILA PALMER GWATKIN

My dear Offy,—   Saltram, Sept. 18, 1783.

I am very much mortified that I could not
stay at Port Elliot till your arrival, which I hear
will be on Saturday, but it would disarrange all
our schemes. Mr. Burke wishes to get to town as
soon as possible. I have full as great a desire to be
there.

If I was to quit Mr. Burke I should have no
excuse left for not visiting all my friends, which
would take up at least a fortnight longer. However, I hope to see Mr. Gwatkin and yourself in
London this next winter, with your daughter,
whom I long much to see.[2]

Mr. and Mrs. Burke and Mr. R. Burke desire
their compliments. They are more than contented
with Port Elliot, and the kind and polite attention

---

1 From Leslie and Taylor, ii, 418 *et seq.* The definite date is
ascertained from the original in the possession of R. G. Gwatkin,
Esq., of Potterne, Devizes.
2 Theophila Gwatkin, the original of Sir Joshua's "Simplicity".

they met with from that family.¹ I intended writing to you from London, and have still a frank for that purpose; but you know what a bad correspondent I am, therefore I hope you will never interpret my neglect to want of that affection which I shall ever have for my dearest Offy.

Yours sincerely,

J. REYNOLDS.

My love to Mr. Gwatkin, and, if he will not come to see me next year, I will come to see him in Cornwall.

LXXII²

To LORD HARDWICKE

My Lord   Dec 5ᵗʰ 1783

May I presume to beg a particular favour of your Lordship—I have a Nephew at Cambridge³ who wishes to take orders, but he wants the qualification necessary, which is a curacy in the Diocese of Ely, without such qualification, or a recom-

---

1 Edward Eliot (1727–1804), who became Baron Eliot in 1784.
2 From the hitherto unpublished original in the British Museum (Add. MSS. 35,350, f. 49).
3 John Palmer (1752–1827), later Hon. Canon of Lincoln. In 1778 he had received the degree of A.B. from St John's College, Cambridge, and had just become Master of Arts.

mendation to the Bishop, whom he has not the honour of knowing, he will probably not be so soon ordained as he wishes, he having a Living promised him immediatly on that event.—What I would request of your Lordship is a Line to your Lordships Brother[1] to desire if my Nephew—Mr Palmer has every other requisite that he would dispense with his want of a Curacy in Cambridgeshire

I hope your Lordship will pardon the liberty which I have taken

I am with the greatest respect

Your Lordships
most humble
and most obedient servant

JOSHUA REYNOLDS

P.S.
Mr Palmer is now in Town
and if His Lordship pleases
would be glad to carry a
line from His Lordship to his Brother the Bishop[2]

---

1 James Yorke (1730–1808), Bishop of Ely from 1781.
2 Sir Joshua's letter was forwarded to the Bishop with the following note:
"Dear Brother.   Decr 7th 83
"Be so good as to let me Know what Answr I shall make to Sir Joshua. He is One I wd willingly oblige if I could.
H."

107

LXXIII[1]

To [CHARLES] SMITH

[1783.]

Sir Joshua Reynolds presents his Compliments to Mr. Smith and has sent a letter of introduction to Lord Macartney.[2] if the direction is not right he may write another himself and seal it before it is deliverd.

LXXIV[3]

To THOMAS ASTLE

Dear Sir,   London, March 8th, 1784.

I am very much flattered by your kind communication of that part of your work which relates to Paintings, and Illuminations, which I have read

---

1 From the hitherto unpublished original in the Boston Public Library. The recipient was probably Charles Smith (1749?–1824), "painter to the Great Mogul", who was in India in 1783 and 1784. He was a nephew of Caleb Whitefoord. *Cf. post*, Letter LXXXII.

2 George Macartney, first Earl Macartney (1737–1806), Governor and President of Fort St George (Madras), 1780–1786. He sat to Sir Joshua in 1764.

3 From Leslie and Taylor, ii, 428, altered in accordance with the part of the text printed in Sotheby's catalogue for a sale on July 5, 1900. The recipient (1735–1803), antiquary and palaeographer, published in this year his most famous work, *The Origin and Progress of Writing*. In Chapter VIII he discusses the paintings, ornaments, and illuminations in old books.

with great pleasure and improvement. I can easily perceive that it will be a learned and accurate work, my studies have been very little in that line, consequently [I] cannot throw in even a mite of assistance.

I am, with the greatest respect,

Your most humble and obedient servant,

J. REYNOLDS.

I don't know whether it is generally known that the word Limner is a corruption of Illuminators. Painters in Miniature in Water-colours are still called Limners with propriety, the vulgar as improperly called us, [painters in oil, Limners.][1]

LXXV[2]

To [STEPHEN FULLER]

Dear Sir   Leicesterfields April 8th 1784

I have the pleasure to inform you that the Academicians have unanimously given the

1 Johnson defines *limner* as "a painter, a picture-maker". The *New Eng. Dict.* gives the same definition, but adds: "Sometimes *spec.*, a water-colour artist".

2 From the hitherto unpublished original in the possession of the Pennsylvania Historical Society. I assume that the recipient was Stephen Fuller, London Agent for the Jamaica House of Assembly. *Cf.* Leslie and Taylor, ii, 442.

preference to Mr. Bacons[1] model for the statue of Lord Rodney—he intends waiting on you to-morrow to receive your further orders.

I am with the greatest respect
Your most obedient
humble servant

J REYNOLDS

LXXVI[2]

To the DUKE OF RUTLAND

London, September 24, 1784.

...I beg leave to return my most sincere thanks for the kind letter which I had the honour of receiving yesterday, and particularly to thank your Grace for your good intention towards my nephew.[3] I am very sensible that even in your high situation you cannot always serve those whom you most wish to serve, but I was so thoroughly

---

1 John Bacon, R.A. (1749–1799). At a meeting of the Council on February 27 two letters from Jamaica were read, in which a request was made that the Academy select a sculptor to design a statue of Lord Rodney, whose defeat of Count de Grasse two years before had protected Jamaica from the French.

2 From *Rutland*, iii, 138 *et seq.*

3 Joseph Palmer (*cf. ante*, Letter xxvi), who had been given an Irish living by Lord Townshend and wished to be advanced. On February 11 Rutland had been appointed Lord Lieutenant of Ireland.

persuaded of your Grace's good inclinations, that though I have solicited every Lord Lieutenant that has gone to Ireland, I have not said anything to your Grace, from a certain confidence that when an opportunity offered my nephew would not be forgot.

Your Grace's picture is finished, and I will immediately make the alteration required in Lord Chatham's picture, and send them both to Belvoir Castle.[1]

I dined with Lady Lucan last Sunday, who told me of her intention of painting a picture for your Grace, but was undetermined what it should be. I shall call on her tomorrow to acquaint her with what your Grace wishes about the Protector Duke of Somerset's picture,[2] which I should think would be the best thing for her to do. I question her success in an historical picture.

In regard to the Nativity,[3] the falling off of the colour must be occasioned by the shaking in the carriage, but as it now is in a state of rest, it will remain as it is for ever; what it wants, I will next year go on purpose to mend it, and from Belvoir

1 There is no record of Rutland's possessing his own portrait by Sir Joshua. John Pitt, second Earl of Chatham (1756–1835), sat in 1779.
2 Edward Seymour, first Earl of Hertford and Duke of Somerset (1506?–1551/2), "Protector of the Realm" from 1546/7 to 1549.
3 The design for the central part of the West Window at New College, Oxford (*cf. ante*, Letter XLIII). It was destroyed in the great fire at Belvoir Castle in 1816.

I should be glad to proceed to Ireland, but I heard yesterday from Mrs. Siddons such a sad account of the Liberty Boys,[1] that I have hardly courage to venture. She came away in a terrible fright, and has not yet recovered herself.

The place which I have the honour of holding, of the King's principal painter, is a place of not so much profit, and of near equal dignity with His Majesty's rat catcher.[2] The salary is £38 per annum, and for every whole length I am to be paid £50, instead of £200 which I have from everybody else. Your Grace sees that this new honour is not likely to elate me very much. I need not make any resolution to behave with the same familiarity as I used to with my old acquaintance....

1 In July Rutland had received a petition which demanded among other things protection for trade, liberty of press, and more equal representation. In September one writer remarked: "Ireland continues nearly in its usual track,...clamorous for liberty, yet more and more discontented as liberty expands itself over that island". (*European Magazine*, VI, 173.)

2 His predecessor Ramsay had died August 11. In 1782 His Majesty's Rat-killer, F. Schomberg, received a salary of £48. 3*s*. 4*d*., so that Sir Joshua's statement is more than an idle jest. *V.* the *Royal Kalendar...for...*1782, 75.

LXXVII¹

To the Right Reverend JONATHAN SHIPLEY

My Lord   London Sep 25. 1784

Your Lordships congratulation on my succeeding Mʳ. Ramsay I take very kindly but it is
a most miserable office, it is reduced from two
hundred, to thirty eight pounds per annum, the
Kings Rat catcher I believe is a better place, and
I am to be paid for the Pictures only a fourth part
of what I have from other people, so that the Portraits of their Majesties are not likely to be better
done now, than they used to be, I should be ruined
if I was to paint them myself.²

I thank your Lordship for your kind invitation
to Chilbolton,³ but I fear it is impracticable this
year, It is not impossible but next year I may have
the honour of waiting on your Lordship at Sᵗ.
Asaph, If I go to Ireland I certainly will go that

1 From a photostat of the hitherto unpublished original recently
  sold by Myers & Co. The recipient (1714–1788), Bishop
  of St Asaph from 1769, sat to Sir Joshua in 1776. The pocket-
  book for 1784 reveals that he was in London in the spring,
  during which time he entertained Sir Joshua at least six times.
2 It was the custom to train one's pupil to manufacture portraits
  of the King and Queen, which were presented to "ambassadors
  and potentates". *Cf.* Leslie and Taylor, ii, 449, n. 2.
3 Shipley spent much of his time at Twyford, near Chilbolton,
  in the northern part of Hampshire. He was rector of Chilbolton from 1761.

way. I have just receivd an Invitation from the
Duke of Rutland either to come this year or the
next, if he stays there so long, of that he seems to
have some doubt, M^{rs}. Siddons who is just returned gives a most terrible account of the
liberty boys. they pelted the Duke and Dutchess
all the time the Play was acting. She receivd a
great many blows which were intended she believes for them, however of this she is not sure,
she considers herself as having had a very narrow
escape from being tarred and featherd, She receivd Letters that this would certainly be [the]
case unless she gave a certain portion of her profits
to the Poor, to this request she was not likely to
comply and was therefore privately conceild for
three day[s] in the house of the Dutchess of
Leinster from whence she retired to Cork in great
fear, being told that at every avenue of Dublin a
watch was set to catch her. It was impossible in
the midst of her narration which she made very
pathetic, to prevent smiling every now and then
when the Words tarring & feathering were repeated with such solemnity as if she thought there
were no words in the English language that would
excite so much horror, this is certainly very excusable in a person that has been so much
frightend at it, but I cannot help smiling this
minute at the Idea of M^{rs}. Siddons being Tarred
& featherd.

The punishment threatend to the Duke of Rut-

land is to cut off his Ears, and she says that two
or three times he has very narrowly escaped falling
into their hands, this mode of punishment has not
much more heroic sound than the other, however it
is seriously terrible to think even of the possibility
of such a thing happening M^{rs}. Siddons thinks
he is in real danger

I beg my most respectfull Compliments to M^{rs}.
Shipley and all the family

and am with the greatest respect
Your Lordships most humble
and most obedient servant

JOSHUA REYNOLDS

LXXVIII¹

To WILLIAM ROSCOE

[(?) 1784.]²

...I am now to return you my thanks for the
present of your poetical works, which I have read
with the greatest pleasure. It is approaching to

1 From Roscoe's *Life of William Roscoe*, London, 1833, i, 34. The
recipient (1753–1831), later the biographer of Lorenzo de'
Medici, had in 1773 been one of the founders of a Liverpool
society for the encouragement of the arts. In 1777 he had
published *Mount Pleasant, a descriptive Poem*, and *An Ode on the
Institution of a Society of Art in Liverpool*.
2 The letter must be dated some time between 1777, when the
poems mentioned in the previous note were first published, and
October, 1784, when Letter LXXIX in this collection was written.

impertinence, to say that I was much surprised at seeing such excellence in a work which I had never heard of before, or the author's name reached my ears; however, I found other people were not quite so ignorant. I mentioned the poem to Mr. Mason,[1] who dined with me a few days ago. I do not recollect that he knew your name, but he was well acquainted with the poem, which he read when it was first published. I had the satisfaction of hearing my opinion fully confirmed by his authority....

LXXIX[2]

To WILLIAM ROSCOE

[October, 1784.]

...I am very glad to hear of the success of your exhibition, and shall always wish to contribute to it to the best of my power.[3]...

1 William Mason (1724–1797), the poet, for whose translation of Du Fresnoy's *Art of Painting* Sir Joshua had written notes (*v. ante*, p. 100, n. 3). In 1784 Mason dined with Sir Joshua on May 21 and September 26.
2 From Roscoe's *Life of William Roscoe*, i, 64.
3 Roscoe, Daulby, and others had in this year revived the Society for promoting Painting and Design in Liverpool. Sir Joshua was represented in the second exhibition.

LXXX[1]

To [the Right Reverend JONATHAN SHIPLEY]

My Lord   London Oct. 26 1784

I am ashamed of the mistakes which I daily make. The accident of writing Kimbolton insteed of Chilbolton[2] was occasiond by a Gentleman present assuring me that it was spelt with a K, the I and M. followed of course, and having but a moderate opinion of my own memory, and allways in a hurry, I did not give myself the trouble of looking for your Lordship's Letter.

The publication which is consigned to Mr. Burke, is as I understand a plan of an Establishment in India for promoting all knowledge relating to the East, the government, natural history, language, &c.

I remember Sir Francis Bacon advises as a refined piece of art, to mention sometimes in a postscript, as if just recollected what is in reality the chief subject of the Letter.[3] But as I dont love tricks of any kind, I confess to your Lordship that my chief reason of writing now is in consequence

1 From the hitherto unpublished original in the possession of W. M. Elkins, Esq., of Philadelphia.
2 *V. ante,* p. 113, n. 3.
3 "I knew one, that when he wrote a Letter, he would put that which was most Materiall, in the *Post-script,* as if it had been a By-matter." (*Of Cunning,* ed. Arber, London, 1871, 439.)

117

of meeting lately the Burkes, we were talking of the cause of the Dean of S Asaph[1] being to be argued next next term in the Kings-bench, and from thence talked of the great advantage it would be if young Richard—Mr Burkes son was engaged in a cause of so great importance and public attention.

I thought afterwards that as many thing are not done, not because they were thought improper but merely from not being thought off, I would take the liberty of mentioning this to your Lordship. I confess I should be extremely happy, if by such an accident as this I should be the means, through your Lordship, of giving an opportunity of bring-ing into public notice a young man of whose abilities I have the highest opinion, it may be some-thing too, that he will of course have the assistance of the abilities of that extraordinary family.

I trust your Lordship will excuse the liberty I have taken, even tho it approaches, as I fear it does, to impertinence in recommending a young advocate in a matter of so great consequence but

---

1 The recipient's son, William Davies Shipley (1745–1826), who was responsible for having reprinted a pamphlet written by his brother-in-law, Sir William Jones, which explained to the uneducated the evils of representation. Because of this, he was prosecuted for libel. After two preliminary trials the case was heard before the Court of King's Bench at the beginning of Michaelmas Term (November 8), where he was finally ac-quitted. *V.* T. B. Howell's *State Trials*, London, 1816, xxi, 847 *et seq.*

1784] *To* [THE RIGHT REV. JONATHAN SHIPLEY]

I am confident if he has the opportunity he will acquit himself with honour to himself and to yr. Lordships satisfaction

I am with the greatest respect

Your Lordships most obedient servant

JOSHUA REYNOLDS.

LXXXI[1]

To WILLIAM ROSCOE

Dear Sir   London Nov 19. 1784

I have receiv'd the Landskip perfectly safe, I do not remember being told by anybody that it had receiv'd any damage on its arrival at Liverpool. M[r]. Pack[2] called on me a few days since to desire I would lend him a picture to copy for his improvement; about three or four years ago I lent him many for that purpose, and he used to bring me his works from the life, in order to be told their faults, as he was only one of many that did the same, I did not recollect his name, nor am I sure I ever knew it. If all those whom I have endeavourd to help forward by lending them pictures and telling them their faults should do me the honour of calling themselves my scholars, I should

1 From the hitherto unpublished original in the possession of W. Westley Manning, Esq., of London.
2 F. Christopher Pack (*b.* 1750), historical, portrait, and landscape-painter, a native of Norwich, who had come to London in 1781.

have the greatest school that ever Painter had. If those young Painters think that from such an inter-course they have a right to say they are my scholars, they are very welcome, I have no kind of objection to it. There is certainly no great harm done in their endeavouring to produce a prejudice in their favour. If I may without vanity suppose this to be the reason of their wishing such an opinion to be entertained in the Country, and as you see, it is not entirely without some foundation.

I return you many thanks for your kind intention of speaking to M^r. J^n. Tarlton ab[out]¹ the Picture when he returns from France.

> I am with the greatest respect
> your most faithfull and
> obedient servant
>
> J REYNOLDS.

LXXXII²

To CHARLES SMITH

Dear Sir,   London, Dec. 3, 1784.

I take this opportunity of returning you my sincere thanks for the present you was so obliging

1 MS. torn. John Tarleton (*b.* 1755), brother of Sir Banastre Tarleton whom Sir Joshua painted in 1782, resided in Liverpool.
2 From Northcote, ii, 209 *et seq.*, altered in accordance with the part of the text printed in Sotheby's catalogue for a sale held June 4, 1907. Perhaps Smith sent the present in return for Sir Joshua's letter of introduction. *Cf. ante*, Letter LXXIII.

as to send me of the yellow colour, which is certainly very beautiful, and I believe will do very well in oil, though perhaps better with water.

I hope you meet with the success you so well deserve. I am only concerned that you are so much out of the way of making that improvement which your Genius would certainly have enabled you to make, if you had staid in England. A painter who has no rivals, and who never sees better works than his own, is but too apt to rest satisfied, and not take what appears to be a needless trouble, of exerting himself to the utmost, pressing his Genius as far as it will go.[1]

I saw the other day, at Mr. Bromil's,[2] a picture of a child with a dog, which, after a pretty close examination, I thought my own painting; but it was a copy, it seems, that you made many years ago.

I am with great respect,

Your most obedient humble servant,

JOSHUA REYNOLDS.

1 "If I had never seen any of the works of Correggio, I should never perhaps have remarked in nature the expression which I find in one of his pieces; or if I had remarked it, I might have thought it too difficult or perhaps impossible to be executed." (*Works*, i, p. lii.)
2 William Brummell, father of the famous "Beau". Sir Joshua's pocket-book shows an engagement at his house for the evening of May 11.

LXXXIII[1]

To Miss [MARY] HAMILTON

*Leicesterfields Friday [January, 1785.][2]

Sir Joshua Reynolds presents his Compliments to Miss Hamilton and begs to know if any time between three and four o'clock to day would be convenient for him to wait on her.

LXXXIV[3]

To the DUKE OF RUTLAND

London, May 30, 1785.

...I hope your Grace will never think that it was want of respect has made me so long defer answering your letter. I waited till the Exhibition opened, in order to see the works of the landskip

1 From the hitherto unpublished original in my possession. The recipient was doubtless Mary Hamilton (1756–1816), only child of Sir William's brother Charles, who married John Dickenson in June, 1785. She it was whom Sir Joshua pictured whenever he read of a beautiful woman in a novel. (*The Farington Diary*, iii, London, 1924, 222.)

2 The note was probably written in the early part of this year, when Sir Joshua was renovating his portrait of Sir William which had just been presented to Miss Hamilton by the sitter. The painter's fee for this service was a kiss. *V. Mary Hamilton*, ed. Anson, London, 1925, 269.

3 From *Rutland*, iii, 211 *et seq.*

painters. The person I fixed on to send to Ireland I had not till lately an opportunity of speaking to on the subject.

Mr. Webber[1] is the person who has accepted the proposal, and intends setting out for Ireland in about three weeks. He is much in the habit of taking views from Nature, some of which are in the Exhibition, which he did from drawings he made when he was with Captain Cook;[2] they are excellent pictures, and I am sure your Grace will approve of his manner of painting. The picture of Rubens' Wife was sold at a greater price than it was worth. It was not one of Rubens' best works, and there was a seperation of the pannel on which it was painted from top to bottom, which had been ill mended.

We are going to erect a monument to the memory of Dr. Johnson; we have all subscribed two guineas each. I will, in consequence of what your Grace has said, take the liberty of putting down your name for that sum.[3]

I acquainted Lady Lucan with your Grace's request in your own words, as they were so flat-

1 John Webber, R.A. (1752–1793), son of a Swiss sculptor. He was represented in the exhibition this year by eight oriental landscapes.
2 James Cook (1728–1779), famous circumnavigator. Webber had accompanied him on his last expedition to the South Seas, returning in 1780.
3 Rutland's name does not appear in the list of subscribers printed in the *Gentleman's Magazine* for January, 1790 (lx, i, 3 *et seq.*).

tering to her Ladyship. She answered that she should set about it immediatly, as she has now found a picture of the Protector Duke of Somerset, which is in the possession of the Marquis of Buckingham, but she says it is but an indifferent picture, and she fears her copy will be no great ornament to your cabinet.[1]

I don't know how to give a description of my Venus, as it is called;[2] it is no more than a naked woman sitting on the ground leaning her back against a tree, and a boy peeping behind another tree. I have made the landskip as well as I could in the manner of Titian. Though it meets with the approbation of my friends, it is not what it ought to be, nor what I should make it. The next I paint I am confident will be better.

I have begun a whole length of the Duc de Chartres[3] for the Prince of Wales, and the Prince is to sit for him. I have sent a head of the Prince to the Exhibition, which I hear is much approved off. He dined with the Academy at our great dinner before the opening of the Exhibition, as did likewise the Duc de Chartres. The Prince behaved

1 *V. ante*, p. 108. George Nugent-Temple-Grenville, first Marquis of Buckingham (1753–1813), second son of George Grenville, the statesman, had been one of Rutland's predecessors as Lord Lieutenant of Ireland and was destined to succeed him.

2 "Venus and Cupid", which was exhibited this year as "Venus". (Graves and Cronin, 1222.)

3 The famous Philippe Égalité (1747–1793).

with great propriety; we were all mightily pleased
with him. I am sorry—*spatiis exclusus iniquis*[1]—
I have only room to say that I shall take care to
execute your Grace's orders respecting the picture
of the young lords when it comes from the Exhibition.[2] ...

LXXXV[3]

To the DUKE OF RUTLAND

July 5, 1785.

...I wish I could express the gratitude I feel
for your Grace's kindness to me in interesting yourself so much in my business, which I think is likely
to turn out very successfull.

In regard to the subject of Mr. Beyers' letter,
I would by all means recommend your Grace to
close with it.[4] Though two thousand pounds is a
great sum, a great object of art is procured by it,
perhaps a greater than any we have at present in

1 Virgil's *Georgics*, IV, 147.
2 The picture of Rutland's three sons, Lords Charles, Robert, and
   William Manners. *Cf. post*, p. 137, n. 2.
3 From *Rutland*, iii, 221 *et seq.*
4 James Byres, agent in Rome for the Duke of Rutland, wrote on
   June 10, that he was now able to purchase for him "The Seven
   Sacraments" by Nicholas Poussin, which at that time were in
   the Bonapaduli Palace. He had arranged to substitute copies
   for the originals so that the papal authorities would not realize
   their loss. *V. Rutland*, iii, 214; *cf.* also *id.* 8.

this nation. Poussin certainly ranks amongst the first of the first rank of painters, and to have such a set of pictures of such an artist will really and truly enrich the nation. I have not the least scruple about the sending copies for originals, not only from the character of Beyers, but if that trick had been intended, he would not have mentioned a word about his having copies made. I don't wish to take them out of your Grace's hands, but I certainly would be glad to be the purchaser myself. I only mean that I recommend only what I would do myself. I really think they are very cheap.

Mr. Webber has declined undertaking his intended journey to Ireland, and that partly by my advice. I found he misunderstood your Grace's intention, which was, as I apprehend, to give him your protection and encouragement so far as employing for six pictures; he, I find, expected that his expences would be defrayed besides paying for those pictures; in short, I thought it would be a troublesome business, and that it would be better to have done with it.

Madame la Comtesse Genlis is just arrived.[1] I had the honour of her company yesterday to dinner. She speaks English tolerably well, and has very pleasing manners. To-day she is gone to Windsor, the Queen having sent to desire to see her....

1 Stéphanie-Félicité Ducrest de Saint-Aubin, Comtesse de Genlis (1746–1830), famous bluestocking.

1785]   *To* THE DUKE OF RUTLAND

Postscript.—I perfectly agree with your Grace that they should be sent as they are, without being cleaned or varnished.[1]

LXXXVI[2]

To JAMES BOSWELL

[July 7, 1785.]

...I am obliged to you for carrying me yester-day to see the execution at Newgate of the five malefactors. I am convinced it is a vulgar error, the opinion that it is so terrible a spectacle, or that it any way implies a hardness of heart or cruelty of disposition, any more than such a disposition is implied in seeking delight from the representation of a tragedy. Such an execution as we saw, where

1 In his letter referred to above Byres wrote: "They must all of them be lined and cleaned".

2 From Leslie and Taylor, ii, 588 *et seq.*, where the original is described as a rough draft. The definite date is ascertained from the fact that on July 6 Sir Joshua, accompanied by Boswell, attended the execution of Peter Shaw, formerly a servant of Burke, who was hanged for robbing. The following day *The Public Advertiser* (copied July 8 by *The Morning Chronicle*) made the following comment: "The first person who appeared upon the scaffold was Mr. Boswell. *That* was nothing extraordinary, but it was surprising when he was followed by Sir Joshua Reynolds. 'Evil communications corrupt good manners'—it is strange how that hard Scot should have prevailed on the amiable painter to attend so shocking a spectacle". *V.* Whitley's *Artists and their Friends in England*, ii, 52. *Cf.* Northcote, ii, 243 *et seq.*

127

there was no torture of the body or expression of
agony of the mind, but where the criminals, on the
contrary, appeared perfectly composed, without
the least trembling, ready to speak and answer with
civility and attention any question that was proposed, neither in a state of torpidity or insensi-
bility, but grave and composed...I am convinced
from what we saw, and from the report of Mr.
Akerman,[1] that it is a state of suspense that is the
most irksome and intolerable to the human mind,
and that certainty, though of the worst, is a more
eligible state; that the mind soon reconciles itself
even to the worst, when that worst is fixed as fate.
Thus bankrupts...I consider it is natural to desire
to see such sights, and, if I may venture, to take
delight in them, in order to stir and interest the
mind, to give it some emotion, as moderate exercise is necessary for the body. This execution is not
more, though I expected it to be too much. If the
criminals had expressed great agony of mind, the
spectators must infallibly sympathise; but so far
was the fact from it, that you regard with admiration the serenity of their countenances and whole
deportment....

1 Keeper of Newgate. *V.* Boswell's *Life*, iii, 431 *et seq.*

LXXXVII[1]

To the DUKE OF RUTLAND

London, July 19, 1785.

...I set out to-morrow morning for Brussels, and consequently take the liberty of writing to your Grace in the midst of hurry and confusion. I have but just received a catalogue of the pictures which are now on view at Brussels. The Emperor has suppressed sixty-six religious houses, the pictures of which are to be sold by auction. Le Comte de Kageneck[2] informs me the Emperor has selected for himself some of the principal pictures; however, there is one altar-piece which belonged to the Convent of the *Dames Blanches* at Lovain, which is to be sold. The subject is the Adoration of the Magi, ten feet by seven feet eight inches, which I take to be about the size of your picture of Rubens.[3] I do not recollect this picture accurately, and, what is *valde diflendus*, I have no notes to refer to—they are, alas, in your Grace's possession.[4]

---

1 From *Rutland*, iii, 227 *et seq.*
2 Envoy extraordinary and minister plenipotentiary from Austria and Germany (1782–1786).
3 In 1779 Rutland had bought at the Verhulst sale at Brussels Rubens's famous picture of the Virgin and Christ, St Catherine, St Agnes, Christine Marguerite, and other female saints.
4 *Cf. ante*, p. 80, n. 4. About "The Adoration of the Magi" Reynolds had written: "a slight performance. The Virgin holds the Infant but aukwardly, appearing to pinch the thigh". (*Works*, ii, 412.)

This picture, I suspect, is the only one worth purchasing if your Grace has any such intention, or will honour me with discretionary orders in regard to other pictures. I shall leave orders for your letter to be forwarded to me at Brussels. The sale does not begin till the twelveth of September; during the whole month of August the pictures are shut up, but for what reason I cannot imagine. The principal object of my journey is to re-examine and leave a commission for a picture of Rubens of a St. Justus—a figure with his head in his hands after it had been cut off—as I wish to have it for the excellency of its painting;[1] the oddness of the subject will, I hope, make it cheap. Whether it will be a bargain or not I am resolved to have it at any rate. I have taken the liberty to take Mr. Crab's verses[2] with me, having but just now received your Grace's letter in which they were contained. I shall have time to examine them critically on the road. I shall have the honour of writing to your Grace again from Brussels....

1 "Every part of this picture is touched in such a style that it may be considered as a pattern for imitation." (*Works*, ii, 328 *et seq.*)
2 Possibly the *Lines on Belvoir Castle*. *V.* Huchon's *Crabbe*, Paris, 1906, 226 n. The poet was Rutland's chaplain.

LXXXVIII[1]

To the DUKE OF RUTLAND

Leicester Fields, July 20, 1785.

...Lord Lucan,[2] who is just about setting out for Ireland, will present to your Grace the picture which Lady Lucan has made of the Protector Duke of Somerset.

The landskip painter, Mr Webber, which I have engaged, is at least equal [to], I think better than, Marlow.[3] In regard to my visiting Ireland this summer, I am loth to abandon the idea; at the same time it appears impossible, when I consider the quantity of work which I have before me.

May I now beg your Grace's indulgence and sollicit your interest in a matter which relates to myself. I believe I mentioned to your Grace the reduction of the salary of the King's Painter from two hundred to fifty pounds per annum.[4] As there is great difficulty of having the old salary restored, as it would open the door to such numerous sollicitations, I thought there was an oppertunity of giving me a very honourable compensation in making me secretary and register to the Order of

1 From *Rutland*, iii, 229.
2 Charles Bingham (1735–1799), created in 1776 Baron Lucan of Castlebar, co. Mayo.
3 William Marlow (1740–1813), who had been Sir Joshua's neighbour in Leicester Fields.
4 *Cf. ante*, Letter LXXVI, where his salary is given as £38 *per annum*.

the Bath. Upon this ground, by means of Mr.
Elliot,[1] I asked for it, but it was too late; Mr. Pitt
had already promised it to Mr. Lake,[2] a gentleman
who has some office in the Treasury. Since this
negociation, Mr. Lake has been appointed one of
the Commisioners of Accounts, a place of a thousand a year for life, and is supposed to be incompatible with his holding this place of secretary,
etc.; at the same time, this latter is only three
hundred a year, so that there can be no doubt, if
he can hold only one, which he will keep. I have
therefore to entreat your Grace to procure from
Mr. Pitt that in case Mr. Lake relinquishes it,
I may be the next oars.[3]

If your Grace had been in London when Mr.
Whithead[4] dyed, I should not have despaired of
having had the first promise. I have very little
confidence in Mr. Elliot's interest, and therefore
have not made a second application to him.

Though, as I said before, the difficulties of my
visiting Ireland are very great, yet in this case, if
your Grace can procure me this honourable place,
I should think it an indispensible duty to make my
personal appearance to return my thanks with

1 Edward Eliot, who had accompanied Pitt to France two years
  before and was about to marry Lady Harriot, Pitt's sister.
2 John Martyn Leake, one of the chief clerks in the Treasury.
3 The position, relinquished by Leake, was given to William
  Fauquier.
4 William Whitehead (1715–1785), poet laureate, the previous
  incumbent, had died April 14.

the order about my neck, though not on my shoulder.

Mr. Pitt, I fear, has not much attention to the arts;[1] if he had, he would think it reasonable that a man who had given up so much of his time to the establishment of an Academy, and had attended sixteen years without any emolument whatever, and who unluckily when made the King's Painter was the first person in that place who had their salary reduced to a fourth part, that he should have some compensation. I am confident your Grace would have seen it in this light had the place been in your gift, but a thousand apologies are necessary for my presuming to hope for your Grace's influence with Mr. Pitt in my behalf....

LXXXIX[2]

To the DUKE OF RUTLAND

London, August 22, 1785.

...I set out for Brussells the day after I wrote to your Grace, but left word that if any answer arrived [it was] to be sent after me, but my stay

[1] "It has often been charged against Mr. Pitt that during his long administration he did nothing to encourage Literature or the Fine Arts, or to reward those men who were rising to eminence in those walks of life. I am bound to say that I consider this charge to be well-founded." (Stanhope's *Pitt*, iv, London, 1861, 408.)

[2] From *Rutland*, iii, 234 *et seq.*

abroad was so short that I missed it; however, I have since receivd it in London. I was much disappointed in the pictures of the suppresed religious houses; they are the saddest trash that ever were collected together. The Adoration of the Magi, and St. Justus, by Rubens, and a Crucifixion by Vandyck, were the only tolerable pictures, but these are not the best of those masters. I did not like the Justus as well [as] I did before, but I think of sending a small commission for it; the two others I dare say will not go to above £200 each. The Vandyck was in the church of the Dominicaines at Antwerp.[1] I was shewn some of the pictures which were reserved by the Emperor, which were not a jota better than the common run of the rest of the collection.

Though I was disappointed in the object of my journey, I have made some considerable purchases from private collections. I have bought a very capital picture of Rubens of Hercules and Omphale,[2] a composition of seven or eight figures, perfectly preserved, and as bright as colouring can be carried. The figures are rather less than life; the height of the picture, I believe, is not above seven feet. I have likewise a Holy Family, a

1 *V. post*, p. 139, n. 1.
2 "Hercules with a distaff, Omphale chastising him by pinching his ear." (Catalogue of "Ralph's Exhibition", reprinted by Graves and Cronin, 1604, where the other pictures here mentioned are also listed.)

Silenus and Baccanalians, and two portraits, all by Rubens. I have a Virgin and Infant Christ and two portraits by Vandyck, and two of the best huntings of wild beasts, by Snyders and De Vos, that I ever saw. I begin now to be impatient for their arrival, which I expect every day. The banker, Mr. Danoot, was very ill when we were at Brussels, supposed to be dying; if that should happen his pictures will be sold.[1]

There are no pictures of Mieris[2] either at Antwerp or Brussels. All the pictures in those two places which were worth bringing home I have bought—I mean of those which were upon sale— except indeed one, the Rape of Sabines, for which they asked £3,500; excepting this, I have swept the country, and for this I would not exchange my Hercules and Omphale.

I return Mr. Crabb's verses with many thanks, and many apologies I ought to make for the liberty I took in carrying them abroad with me; there are very beautifull lines in it, but it is not so much finishd as some of his other works. If your Grace should choose to send any commision for the altar- piece of Rubens, or for the Vandyck, the sale begins the twelvth of September; you will please to let me know time enough before the sale for the commision to arrive at Brussels....

1 For Danoot's collection *v. Works*, ii, 264 *et seq.*
2 Frans van Mieris (1635–1681).

XC[1]

To the DUKE OF RUTLAND

September 10, 1785.

...Though I have not been so punctual in answering your Grace's letters as I ought, yet I took care that nothing should prevent me from writing to my correspondent in Flanders, to desire he would go so far as four hundred guineas for the Vandyck, and three hundred for the Rubens. I could not in conscience give him a higher commission. Your Grace will certainly have them, I think within the commission. I must beg leave to mention to your Grace the person I have employed in this business; his name is De Gray,[2] a very excellent painter in *chiaro oscuro*, in imitation of *basrelievos*. He paints likewise portraits in oil and in crayons extremely well. He was very civil and attentive to me when I was at Antwerp, and was the means of my purchasing some very fine pictures. He then told me he intended going to Ireland, having been invited by Mr.Cunningham;[3] and I promised to recommend him likewise to your Grace's protection, which I can with a very safe conscience, not only as a very ingenious artist, but a young man of very pleasing manners. I have no

1 From *Rutland*, iii, 240 *et seq.*
2 De Gree (*d.* 1788), a native of Antwerp, Sir Joshua had met on his first trip to Flanders in 1781. He eventually made his home in Ireland.
3 The recipient of Letters XCIV and XCVI?

doubt but he is very happy in this opportunity of doing anything to oblige your Grace, and will be very zealous in the performance.

I don't know how to account for the pictures at Antwerp not appearing so striking to me this last journey as they did the first. I was disappointed in many other pictures besides those on sale.[1] It ought at least to teach me this lesson—not to be very impatient when anyone differs with me about the degree of excellence of any pictures, since I find I differ so much from myself at different times.

I have inclosed the title and that part of the catalogue which has the Rubens and the Vandyck, which I apprehend is all that your Grace wished to see.

The picture will be sent away on Monday by way of Liverpool.[2] In the hurry of pictures I have

1 "On viewing the pictures of Rubens a second time, they appeared much less brilliant than they had done on the former inspection. He could not for some time account for this circumstance; but when he recollected, that when he first saw them, he had his note-book in his hand, for the purpose of writing down short remarks, he perceived what had occasioned their now making a less impression in this respect than they had done formerly. By the eye passing immediately from the white paper to the picture, the colours derived uncommon richness and warmth. For want of this foil, they afterwards appeared comparatively cold." (Note by Malone in *Works*, i, lxxii *et seq.*)

2 The portrait of Lords Charles, Robert, and William Manners. In his account-book Sir Joshua wrote: "Duke of Rutland for his three sons sent to Ireland, September, 1785, £300". (Graves and Cronin, 614 *et seq.*)

neglected thanking your Grace for your kind
sollicitations in my favour with Mr. Pitt. I am, as
I certainly ought to be, as grateful as if it had been
crowned with success.[1]

If your Grace wishes to remain longer in Ireland,
I think I may congratulate you on losing the Irish
propositions.[2] If they had passed it is most certain
there would have been a great commotion here by
addresses from the manufacturers and inflam-
matory speeches to mobbs, that would probably
have gone near to shake the Administration; but
now all is quiet and settled again.. . .

XCI[3]

To the DUKE OF RUTLAND

London, September 22, 1785.

. . .I am sorry to acquaint your Grace that
there is nothing bought at the sale. I have inclosed
Mr. De Gree's letter, by which it appears they went
much above even the commission that you wished
me to send. I cannot think that either the Rubens
or Vandyck were worth half the mony they sold for.
The Vandyck was an immense picture and very

1 *Cf. ante*, Letter LXXXVIII.
2 The twenty propositions passed by Parliament, respecting
Ireland's right of legislating for itself, had been defeated on
August 12. *V. Gentleman's Magazine*, LV, ii, 657.
3 From *Rutland*, iii, 242.

scantily filled; it had more defects than beauties,[1] and as to the Rubens, I think your Grace's is worth a hundred of them. They are so large, too, that it would cost near two hundred pounds bringing them to England. I have sent the catalogue to Lord Sydney's[2] office to be forwarded to your Grace....

XCII[3]

To the DUKE OF RUTLAND

London, September 26, 1785.

...Immediatly on the receipt of your Grace's letter I wrote to Mr. De Gree to make enquiry to whom the pictures were sold, and whether they would part with them again at a certain profit; at the same time, I am confident if your Grace saw them you would not be very anxious about possessing them. The Poussin's[4] are a real national object, and I rejoice to hear that the scheme of their coming to England is in such forwardness.

1 "For its defects ample amends is made in the Christ, which is admirably drawn and coloured." (*Works*, ii, 298.)
2 Thomas Townshend, first Viscount Sydney (1733–1800), the "Tommy Townshend" of Goldsmith's *Retaliation*, at this time Pitt's Secretary of State for the Home Department.
3 From *Rutland*, iii, 244.
4 The "Seven Sacraments". *Cf. ante*, p. 125, n. 4.

Mr. Boswell has just sent me his "Johnsoniana",[1]
which is one of the most entertaining books I ever
read. If your Grace pleases I will send it by the
same conveyance as the catalogue. I think you
will be agreably amused for a few hours; there are
Johnson's opinions upon a great variety of subjects, and Boswell has drawn his character in a
very masterly manner. The Bishop of Killaloo,[2]
who knew Johnson very well, I think will subscribe
to the justness and truth of the drawing....

XCIII[3]

To ANDREW STRAHAN

London: October 23rd, 1785

...As without doubt you wish to make this
New Edition of Johnson's Dicty,[4] as complete as

1 Probably an advance copy of the *Journal of a Tour to the
Hebrides*, which was published on October 1. (*London Chronicle*,
lviii, 300.)
2 Thomas Barnard, D.D. (1728–1806), consecrated Bishop of
Killaloe and Kilfenora in 1780.
3 From catalogue 886 (item 364), issued in June, 1924, by James
Tregaskis, of London. The recipient (1749–1831) was the well-
known publisher.
4 Late in this year the sixth edition was published. In the *London
Chronicle* for October 13–15 (lviii, 362) the proprietors had ad-
vertised that they were about to publish a new edition, and in
the issue for October 25–27 (*id.* 404) they stated that Sir Joshua
had, "with a Liberality which distinguishes his Character, indulged the Proprietors with the Use" of the copy bequeathed
to him by Johnson. No mention, however, is made in this or
subsequent notices (*id.* 452, 510, 535) of Dyer's copy.

possible, I take the liberty of acquainting you, that
Mr. Dyer[1] a friend of Dr. Johnson's had by the
Doctor's desire made notes, explanations and corrections of words to be used, in a future edition;
for this purpose the Dictionary was divided into
four folio volumes, with a certain number of blank
leaves at the end of each volume. Mr. Ed. Burke
(who was likewise an intimate friend of Dyer) is
in possession of those volumes,[2] I mentioned to him
that I believed you would be glad to have the use
of them for your New Edition, to which he readily
consented. If you think this worth your attention
I will desire Mr. Burke to send them to Town.

Mr. Dyer was a very judicious and learned
Critic, and held in the highest estimation in our
Club. I have heard Mr. Burke say that he never
knew a man of more extensive knowledge; not
having published anything his name is not much
known in the world. He overlooked the English
translation of Plutarch and translated some of the
lives from the Original Greek, the old translation
being too bad to use any part of it. . . .

1 Samuel Dyer (1725–1772), an original member of the Club,
whose portrait Sir Joshua painted in 1770 for Burke. When
Tonson brought out a new edition of Plutarch's *Lives* in 1758,
Dyer translated the lives of Pericles and Demetrius and revised
the entire work.

2 Burke's copy of the *Dictionary*, now in the British Museum, is in
the usual two volumes, "with a certain number of blank leaves
at the end of each volume", on which are written Dyer's
additions and corrections.

XCIV[1]

To [EDMUND FRANCIS] CUNNINGHAM

Dear Sir   London Nov. 25 1785

I return you a thousand thanks for your kind attention to my wishes about the two pictures of Rubens at the Capuchins, and you give me some hopes of a possibility of coming at them. I believe what I have offer'd, £300 for the two Pictures, is their full value, they have been much damaged and ill mended. As they are at present they appear to be worth little or nothing. I go upon speculation that I can mend them, and restore them to their original beauty, which if I can accomplish, I shall have got a prize, if they will not clean it will be so much mony thrown away. this is exactly the state of the Case.—In regard to the copies to be made, I will be at that additional expence, I would send over a young Artist who formerly lived with me, for that purpose, and will give him proper directions how to give the copy an old appearance, so

---

1 From the original in my possession. First published in the *Catalogue of the Collection of Autograph Letters...formed...by Alfred Morrison*, v, 1891, 250 *et seq.*, where the recipient is said to be Edmund Francis Cunningham, or Calze (1742?–1795), a portrait-painter, who spent a great part of his life on the continent. The letter is addressed: "a Mons[r] Mons[r] Cunynham/Lille".

that few, even amongst the Connoiseurs shall distinguish the difference.¹

If it is represented to the family by whom the
Picture was given, that they are allmost destroyed
and will soon be totally lost, they may reasonably
think that putting copies in their place, is the best
means of preserving the remembrance of the gift
of their family. That it may not appear that I am
undervalueing the goods which I want to buy
according to the common custom, let me quote
what Monʳ. Michel says of those two Pictures in his
life and account of the Pictures of Rubens.² dans
la seconde chapelle à la gauche de l'entree de
l Eglise de Capucins representant l Adoration des
Bergers, sa Composition est tres-revenante d'un
Coloris vigoreux et savamment groupè, mais helas,
un de ces frotteurs dont l'Universe abonde, a
effacé la superficie de tout l'ouvrage; de maniére
qu'il n'y a laissè que le triste souvenir, qu'autrefois
ce tableau fut du pinceau de le Rubens. Of the
other Picture, Sᵗ. Francis receiving the Enfant
Jesus, he says likewise, ce tableau a encore passé
le maniement décharnant du dernier, car les
draperies de la Vierge, & le fond de tout l'ouvrage,

1 Desenfans, the picture-dealer, once bought as an original a copy
of a Claude painted by Giuseppe Marchi, Sir Joshua's first
pupil. *Cf. post,* p. 216, n. 2.
2 *Histoire de la Vie de P. P. Rubens* . . . par J. F. M. Michel, Bruxelles,
1771, 198 *et seq.* Sir Joshua has omitted two phrases and has, of
course, altered the accents.

est autant qu'emp[orté.] This printed account of the Pictures wil[l be a] sufficient apology both to the Capuchins [and the] family for placing good Copies in the [Church.][1] I calculate the Copies to cost me about £100. When a man is about an object that will upon the whole cost £400 it is not worth while to bogle at small things, if making the principal of the family a compliment of a present of a Gold watch or any English trinket of the value of about twenty Pounds I should be glad to do it I have not left room to make such an apology as I intended for the trouble which I have given to you and express my thankfulness for the great favour you have conferrd on me—

I am with the greatest respect

Yours &

JOSHUA REYNOLDS

XCV[2]

To the DUKE OF RUTLAND

London, December 14, 1785.

. . . Mr. De Gree, the bearer of this, was very desirous of the honour of being introduced to your Grace; I therefore delayed my letter in order to give him this opportunity. Besides being a very

1 The lacunae are caused by a portion of the MS. being torn off with the seal.
2 From *Rutland*, iii, 268.

ingenious artist in a variety of ways, he is a very excellent connoiseur, and was the means of my procuring some very excellent pictures at Antwerp. He was the agent about the pictures of Rubens and Vandyck, consequently he will be able to give your Grace all his information about them.

I am very glad the picture of the children meets with your Grace's approbation; I am sorry to say the companion is not yet finished, but I will endeavour to exert myself and set furiously about it.[1]

The portrait of Morilio which I have seen is very finely painted, and there is not the least doubt about its being an original of his hand; it will be a very considerable acquisition to your Grace's collection. The Poussins, I suppose, I am not to expect for some time; when they arrive I shall certainly take all possible care of them....

XCVI[2]

To [EDMUND FRANCIS] CUNNINGHAM

Dear Sir   London Dec 29th 1785

The great probability there is that the Pictures are beyond the powers of Art to restore, I confess to you, made me repent offering so much as I did

1 *Cf. ante*, p. 137, n. 2. The companion was the portrait of John Henry Granby, Lady Elizabeth Isabella Manners, and Lady Katherine Mary Manners, three of Rutland's children.

2 From a copy of the hitherto unpublished original in the possession of Alfred C. Meyer, Esq., of Chicago.

in my last letter.[1] however as they have declined
accepting it I am very well contented to be cleared
of my engagement; When I offered three hundred
pounds for the two Pictures, I meant I would give
so much to have them safe in my house without
further expence, except the carriage duty &c
which I believe would amount to near forty pounds.
according to their demand, the Pictures would cost
me before I received them upwards of five hundred Guineas. I wish therefore now totally to decline being a purchaser unless they choose to part
with them clear of all deduction for three hundred
pounds. Tho we have not succeeded in this business I am not the less obliged to you for the trouble
and attention you have given to it and should be
very glad of any opportunity of shewing the
gratefull sense I have of your kindness

I beg most respectfull compliments to the Ladies
and am with the greatest respect

Your most humble

and most obedient servant

J REYNOLDS

In regard to the last supper of Lucas of Leyden,
I have the same picture of a larger size. I only
wished to know the name of the Painter. neither
of them I am certain are by Lucas of Leyden.

[1] Letter xciv in this collection.

P S. as you mentioned an intention of becoming a purchaser yourself, I beg leave to observe that tho I have offer'd so great a sum for the Pictures they are by no means worth half that sum to anybody else. I have in my Possession a Picture of Rubens as large as the Nativity which I bought at a public sale in London for twenty five pounds, tho' it was not so much damaged as those pictures are. If both of them were in a sale in London I should [expect]¹ to buy them both for fifty pounds—they are worth nothing, (as I observed in my former letter,) but to a Painter. I should be very sorry therefore if you bought them upon speculation, as I think you would lose considerably by it.

XCVII²

To the DUKE OF RUTLAND

London, January 4, 1786.

...I have begun the copy of Lord Mansfield³ for your Grace. He called on me and spoke himself about it. It is thought one of my best portraits, but he should have sat eight or ten years before; his countenance is much changed since he has lost

---

1 Obliterated in the MS.   2 From *Rutland*, iii, 272.

3 William Murray, first Earl of Mansfield (1705–1793), Lord Chief Justice of the King's Bench, who had sat to Reynolds in 1776. His letter to Rutland concerning this portrait is printed in *Rutland*, iii, 268.

his teeth. I have made him exactly what he is now, as if I was upon my oath to give the truth, the whole truth, and nothing but the truth. I think it necessary to treat great men with this reverence, though I really think his Lordship would not have been displeased if this strict adherence to truth had been dispensed with, and drawn a few years younger. However, being told by everybody what a good picture, and how like it is, he is perfectly pleased with it, and has ordered a print by Bartolozzi to be made after it.

The next picture I take in hand shall be Lord Granby[1] with the Hussar, but I fear it will not be finished till the spring, as I am at present overpowered with business. However, I shall always take care not to neglect your Grace's commands....

XCVIII[2]

To the DUKE OF RUTLAND

London, February 20, 1786.

...I shall take care to obey your Grace's orders about the Velasques[3] and Van der Meulen when they arrive. Lord Mansfield's picture is

---

1 John, Marquess of Granby (1721–1770), father of the recipient. This posthumous portrait, destroyed in the fire at Belvoir Castle, represented Lord Granby leaning on his war-horse with the hussar, John Nötzell, by its side.

2 From *Rutland*, iii, 283.   3 *Cf. post*, p. 152, n. 1.

finished, I mean your Grace's copy. I am now about Lord Granby with the horse and Swiss servant, which I think will be finished in a week's time, and if the reumatism will give me leave, for I am very stiff and awkward at present, I hope in about a fortnight after to finish the children.[1]

I forgot whether I mentioned in my last letter that I have received a commission from the Empress of Russia[2] to paint an historical picture for her, the size, the subject, and everything else left to me; and another on the same conditions for Prince Potemkin. The subject I have fixed on for the Empress is Hercules strangling the serpents in the cradle, as described by Pindar, of which there is a very good translation by Cowley.[3]

My nephew, Mr. Palmer, who is now with me, desires me to make an apology for him, as he came away whilst your Grace was on your tour in the country, and had no opportunity of asking your Grace's leave, which he was in duty bound to do.[4] . . .

---

1 *Cf. ante*, p. 145, n. 1.
2 Catherine II, the Great (1729–1796). Gregory Alexandrovitch, Prince Potemkin (1736–1791), was one of her favourites.
3 *Pindarique Odes*, London, 1669, *The First Nemeaean Ode of Pindar*, 13 *et seq.* The subject was chosen "as the most fit, in allusion to the great difficulties which the Empress of Russia had to encounter in the civilization of her empire, arising from the rude state in which she found it". (Northcote, ii, 215.)
4 *Cf. ante*, p. 110, n. 3.

149

XCIX[1]

To the DUKE OF RUTLAND

London, March 21, 1786.

...Your Grace has made us all very happy by the dignitary which you have been pleased to conferr on my nephew;[2] and, indeed, the manner in which your Grace has been pleased to communicate this intelligence so much enhances the obligation, that I don't know whether the kind expressions with which it is accompanied has not given me as much pleasure as the thing itself. I have not yet heard from Mr. Palmer, but I take it for granted he is the happiest of men.

The only news of virtu at present is Lord Ashburnham's purchace of the collection of the late Humphry Morris,[3] for which he gave four thousand pounds. Out of forty pictures he has reserved, I think, six only, the principal of which are two Salvator Rosa's, a landskip of Nicholas Poussin, and a Mola; the remaining part were sold by auction, which amounted only to four hundred pounds. He has made, in my opinion, a very bad bargain....

1 From *Rutland*, iii, 289.
2 This could not refer to an actual appointment. *Cf. post*, Letters CIV and CVII.
3 Humphry Morice (1723–1785), politician and patron of the arts, had died in Florence on October 18. John, Earl Ashburnham (1724–1812), had been one of the Lords of the Bedchamber to George II.

CI

To the DUKE OF RUTLAND

London, June 23, 1786.

...I am very much flattered by your Grace's kind invitation to Ireland, and very much mortified that it is not in my power to accept of it this year, on account of the picture which I am to paint for the Empress of Russia. However, I don't despair of accomplishing this visit to Ireland before your Grace leaves it.

In regard to the Augustus,[2] I fear it is irretrievably gone. It was bought by the Duke of Portland for £125. The Duke of Marlborough told me he bid as far as £120, but the Duke of Portland was resolved to have it at any price; he made the same resolution respecting the vase,[3] which he bought at 900 guineas. The Augustus would have been worth double what it was sold for if it had been perfect. The lower part of the chin and the

1 From *Rutland*, iii, 311 *et seq.*
2 "a cameo of the head of Augustus Caesar, upon a remarkable fine onyx, the head white, upon a jacinth ground, the workmanship of superlative excellence. It was found at Malta." (*Gentleman's Magazine*, LVI, i, 526.) This and the following item were bought at the sale of the Portland Museum, which had begun May 24 and had ended June 7.
3 "The most celebrated antique vase, or sepulchral urn, from the Barberini cabinet at Rome. It is said to have been the identical urn which contained the ashes of the Rom. Emp. Alexander Severus, and his mother Mammea." (*Id.*)

151

neck was gone; what remained was of the most exquisite Greek workmanship.

I suspect the Pope's head of Velasques to be the same as is in the Pamphili Palace at Rome,[1] and not the portrait of Leo Xth. The same Pope, who having disobliged Guido, he made a caricatura of him—or, rather, made a devil of him—and put him under Michael's feet.[2]

At Chiswick there is likewise a head of the same Pope by Velasques, but not equal to that which is at Rome, which I think is one of the first portraits in the world.

I have heard nothing of the Seven Sacraments. I hope no cross accident has happened. I wish they were safe landed....

---

1 On July 5 Byres wrote from Rome: "I am glad that the Duke has got a fine Velasquez. They are very rare to be met with. . . . That you mention in Rome is in the Doria Panfili Palace. It is likewise a half-length sitting." (*Rutland*, iii, 326.)

2 Sir Joshua's copy of Guido's "St. Michael" is in the Chapel of Hampton Court Palace.

CI[1]

To LORD OSSORY

My Lord   London July 10 1786

After a carefull examination of the Picture I am sorry to confirm Roma's[2] opinion that it has been much damaged and painted upon, and that too in places which can never be successfully repaired particularly in the back of the Venus. I am at a loss what to advise, the Picture cleaner will only make it ten times worse

The best advice I can give is that we make an exchange, by which each of us may have a bargain. If there ever was an instance where an exchange may be[3] made by which both parties may be benefitted, it is the present.

The Picture is a copy by Titian himself from that in the Colonna palace, I am confident I see the true *Titian tint* through the yellow dirty Paint and varnish with which the picture is coverd.

If it was mine I should try to get this off, or ruin the picture in the attempt. It is the colour alone that can make it valuable. The Venus is not hand-

1 From the original in the possession of W. Westley Manning, Esq. First published by Leslie and Taylor (ii, 493 *et seq.*), where the error in the date is due to a misprint.
2 Spiridone Roma (*d.* 1787), an Italian portrait-painter and decorator, often employed to clean pictures.
3 "may be" ends the first page and begins the second. It was not Sir Joshua's practice to use the catch-word.

some and the Adonis is wretchedly disproportioned with an immense long body & short legs. The sky and Trees have been painted over and must be repainted which I have the vanity to think nobody can do but myself—at any rate it is better to let it remain at my house till your Lordship comes to town.

I am with the greatest respect

Your Lordships
most humble and
most obedient servant

J REYNOLDS

P S I am thinking what picture to offer in Exchange—what if I give Gainsboroughs Pigs for it, it is by far the best Picture he ever Painted or perhaps ever will.[1]

---

[1] When Sir Joshua purchased Gainsborough's "Girl and Pigs" at the exhibition in 1782, he sent a flattering note to his rival, who answered that "it could not fail to afford him the highest satisfaction that he had brought his pigs to so fine a market". (Whitley's *Thomas Gainsborough*, London, 1915, 186.)

CII[1]

To the DUKE OF RUTLAND

London, July 13, 1786.

...In regard to the Venus, the Duke of Dorset[2] is to have it, not for himself, but for a French marquis, whose name I have forgot; he is to give me 400 guineas for it. I have since done another with variations, which I think better than the first; but I am not fond of shewing it till the other is disposed of....

CIII[3]

To LORD OSSORY

My Lord,—   London, July 17, 1786.

My mind at present is entirely occupied in contriving the composition of the Hercules, otherwise I think I should close with your Lordship's

1 From *Rutland*, iii, 322.
2 John Frederick Sackville, third Duke of Dorset (1754–1799), at this time ambassador extraordinary and plenipotentiary to the court of France. For the Venus *cf. ante*, p. 124.

"*Sir Joshua's* delicious *Venus*—is gone the way of all flesh—She is sold—and gone to Paris. The *Duke of Dorset* the buyer—though the *French women*, some time since seemed to think, it was *not necessary* to encrease the *female* part of his *Grace's collection*!

"None of *Sir Joshua's* women ever made themselves *cheap*—though this was such as to be *cheap at any price*. The *Duke* had her for four hundred—Others he has had, lost him infinitely *more*!" [Newspaper clipping in Anderdon's copy of Edwards's *Anecdotes*.]
3 From Leslie and Taylor, ii, 494.

155

proposal, which I acknowledge is very flattering to me. There is another proposal which I beg leave to make, which I can execute immediately, and which I think will be equally valuable to your Lordship, and save me a great deal of time, which is to copy the Nymph and Shepherd,[1] with many improvements which I wish to make, and add to it a landskip, to make it the size of her frame at Ampthill: depend upon it I shall make it the most striking picture I ever did.

I am, with the greatest respect,

Your Lordship's most humble
and obedient servant,

J. REYNOLDS.

P.S.—If I paint this picture perfectly to your Lordship's satisfaction, I expect you will give me the shield to the bargain.

CIV[2]

To the DUKE OF RUTLAND

London, August 29, 1786.

...I have the pleasure to acquaint your Grace that the pictures[3] are in the river, and that I am expecting them in Leicester Fields every hour.

---

1 Possibly the "Nymph and Boy" which Ossory chose at Sir Joshua's death. See Graves and Cronin, 1223.

2 From *Rutland*, iii, 340.

3 The "Seven Sacraments." *Cf. post*, Letter CVI.

I should have deferred writing to your Grace till I had been able at the same time to give some account of their merit, but my nephew setting out to-morrow morning for Ireland, and being very desirous of bearing a letter to your Grace, I thought it would be no bad news to communicate this intelligence; the bad part of the story is, that I insured the pictures for two thousand pounds, which cost thirty pounds. I confess I insured them with an ill will, but as I had received your Grace's orders I had no business to consider about the propriety of it.

I beg your Grace's pardon for returning to the subject of my nephew. If I can do nothing for him during your Grace's administration, I must give up all thoughts, or rather he must give up all expectations, from any advantage he is to receive from my interest with the great. We are not so ambitious as to think of bishopricks, but if Dean Marly[1] succeeds to the next bishoprick, which according to report is probable, if your Grace would give to Mr. Palmer his leavings, either his deanery or the living of Loughilly, your Grace would make him at once what you was so good as to say you would do one time or another, *an inde-*

---

1 Richard Marlay, son of Chief Justice Marlay, had been made Dean of Ferns (where Joseph Palmer was Chancellor) in 1769. He became rector of Loughgilly in the diocese of Armagh in 1772 and was raised to the bishopric of Clonfert in 1787. (H. Cotton's *Fasti Ecclesiae Hibernicae, Leinster*, Dublin, 1848, 352.)

pendent gentleman, and I shall never pretend to have any further demands on your Grace on his account. Your Grace some time since wished Marlow,[1] the landskip painter, to come to Dublin, but he has, as I am told, quitted business. I have met lately with a painter of landskips and buildings that I think excells Marlow—Mr. Hodges,[2] who went the first voyage of Captain Cook and has since been in the East Indies. He is now desirous of seing Ireland, and would embark immediatly if he was sure of your Grace's protection. He is a very intelligent and ingenious artist, and produced, I think, the best landskips in the last exhibition, which were taken from drawings which he made in the East Indies....

CV [3]

To LORD OSSORY

My Lord,—   London, Sept. 5, 1786.

I have sent the picture, according to your Lordship's orders, to Mr. Vandergucht,[4] which I was very sorry to do, and I hope my sorrow did not proceed entirely from a selfish motive, for

1 *Cf. ante*, p. 131.
2 William Hodges, R.A. (1744–1797), an imitator of Wilson. He accompanied Cook on the *second* voyage. (Sandby's *History of the Royal Academy*, London, 1862, i, 203.)
3 From Leslie and Taylor, ii, 495 *et seq.*
4 Benjamin Vandergucht (*d.* 1794), picture-dealer and cleaner.

I felt the same sensation when I saw the picture of Vandyke at Wilton,[1] and the Titian at North-umberland House, after they had been cleaned and painted upon: from being pictures of in-estimable value, they are now hardly worth the rank of good copies; however, this is so to painters' eyes only.

Without any disrespect to Mr. Vandergucht, who, as far as I know, may repair the picture as well as any other man of the trade in England, the value of the picture will be lessened in proportion as he endeavours to make it better; and yet much must be done. What I proposed I am still con-fident was a good bargain on both sides; however, it is now over.

I have received the Seven Sacraments of Poussin, which the Duke of Richmond[2] has bought out of the Borrapudule palace at Rome. They are an ex-ceeding fine set of pictures, in perfect condition, having never been touched I believe, not even washed, ever since they were painted; they are consequently very dirty, but it is dirt that is easily washed off. They cost him £2000. I should be glad to give him £500 for his bargain.

I am, with great respect,

Your Lordship's,

J. REYNOLDS.

1 One of the seats of the Earl of Pembroke.
2 A slip of the pen. Rutland is of course meant.

CVI[1]

To the DUKE OF RUTLAND

London, September 7, 1786.

...I have the pleasure to acquaint your Grace that the pictures are arrived safe in Leicester Fields. I hang over them all day, and have examined every picture with the greatest acuracy. I think, upon the whole, that this must be considered as the greatest work of Poussin, who was certainly one of the greatest painters that ever lived.[2]

I must mention, at the same time, that (except to the eye of an artist, who has the habit of seeing through dirt) they have a most unpromising appearance, being incrustated with dirt. There are likewise two or three holes, which may be easily mended when the pictures are lined. Excepting this, which is scarce worth mentioning, they are in perfect condition. They are just as Poussine left them. I believe they have never been washed or va[r]nished since his time. It is very rare to see a picture of Poussine, or, indeed, of any great painter that has not been defaced in some part or rather, and mended by picture cleaners, and have been reduced by that means to half their value.

1 From *Rutland*, iii, 343.
2 His admiration for Poussin is brought out in his fifth *Discourse*. (*Works*, i, 134 *et seq*.) The "Seven Sacraments" are mentioned in his thirteenth *Discourse*, which was delivered this December. (*Works*, ii, 130.)

I expected but seven pictures, but there are eight. The sacriment of Baptism is represented by Christ baptising St. John, but that picture, which does not seem to belong to the sett (though equally excellent with the rest), is St. John baptising the multitude.

I calculate that those pictures will cost your Grace 250 guineas each. I think they are worth double the mony.

A few evenings since I met Lord Besborough[1] at Brooks'. I told him of the arrival of the pictures, and asked him (as he rememberd them very well) what he thought they might be worth. He said they would be cheap at six thousand pounds.

I think Mr. Beyers managed very well to get them out of Rome, which is now much poorer, as England is richer than it was, by this acquisition.

I have likewise made a great purchase of Mr. Jenkins[2]—a statue of Neptune and a Triton grouped together, which was a fountain in the Villa Negroni (formerly Montalto). It is near eight feet high, and reckond Bernini's greatest work. It will cost me about 700 guineas before

---

1 William Ponsonby, second Earl of Bessborough (1704–1793), patron of Nollekens. Brooks's was a fashionable gaming club in St. James's Street.

2 "A notorious dealer in antiques and old pictures, who resided at Rome for that purpose." (Smith's *Nollekens and his Times*, ed. Gosse, London, 1895, 37; *cf.* 222.) Bernini's "Neptune" had received mention in the tenth *Discourse.* (*Works*, ii, 28.) *Cf. post*, Letter cxv.

I get possession of it. I buy it upon speculation, and hope to be able to sell it for a thousand.

The Boccapaduli Palace was visited by all foreigners, merely for the sake of those picture by Poussine, for I do not remember there were any others of any kind. Those Sacriments are much superior to those in the Orleans collection, which I thought were but feebly painted, tho equally excellent for invention. There is arrived in the same case a porto-folio with prints after the works of Raffielle in the Vatican, and some colour'd prints after antient paintings. I saw this morning a very fine picture of Raffielle of a Madonna and Bambino, which Lord Cooper[1] brought from Italy, which he carries back with him again. He sets off for Italy next week, and, I understand, does not intend to return....

CVII[2]

To the DUKE OF RUTLAND

London, October 4, 1786.

...I am very well disposed to fill this letter with expressing the happiness which we all feel from your Grace's kindness towards my nephew;[3] but as I am sure you would rather hear about the

1 George Nassau, third Earl Cowper (1738–1789), who spent most of his life in Florence.   2 From *Rutland*, iii, 346 *et seq.*
3 He was instituted and installed Dean of Cashel on June 22 of the following year. (H. Cotton's *Fasti Ecclesiae Hibernicae*, *Munster*, Dublin, 1851, i, 38.)

pictures, I shall only say we feel it with all the gratitude we ought.

Everything relating to the pictures has hitherto turned out most prosperously. They have past through the operations of lining and cleaning, all which has been performed in my own house under my own eye. I was strongly recommended to a Neopolitan[1] as having an extraordinary secret for cleaning pictures, which, though I declined listening to at first, I was at length persuaded to send for the man, and tried him by putting into his hands a couple of what I thought the most difficult pictures to clean of any in my house. The success was so complete that I thought I might securely trust him with the Sacriments, taking care to be allways present when he was at work. He possesses a liquid which he applies with a soft sponge only, and, without any violence of friction, takes off all the dirt and varnish without touching or in the least affecting the colours. With all my experience in picture cleaning, he really amazed me. The pictures are now just as they came from the easel. I may now safely congratulate your Grace on being relieved from all anxiety. We are safely landed; all danger is over.

The eighth picture, the Baptism of the Multitude, does not belong to the set, nor is it engraved as the rest are. The figures are not upon the same scale; they are of less dimensions. This picture is

1 Biondi, by name. *Cf. post*, Letter CXVI.

the only one that has been in a picture-cleaner's hands, is more damaged, and has been painted upon, but it is equally excellent with the rest.

As to their originality, it is quite out of all question. They are not only original, but in his very best manner, which cannot be said of the set in the Duke of Orleans's collection. Those latter are really painted in a very feeble manner; and, though they are undoubtedly originals, have somewhat the appearance of copies.

Wellbore Ellis Agar[1] told me they were offered to him some years ago for £1,500, but he declined the purchase by the advice of Hamilton, the painter,[2] on account, as he said, of their being in bad condition.

It is very extraordinary that a man so conversant in pictures should not distinguish between mere dirtyness and what is defaced or damaged. Mr. Agar dined with me a few days since,[3] with a party of connoiseurs; but the admiration of the company, and particularly of the good preservation of those pictures, so mortified him at having missed them, that he was for the whole day very much what the vulgar call *down in the mouth*, for he made very little use of it either for eating or talking.

1 One of the commissioners of the customs, whose "exquisite collection of pictures" is mentioned by Boswell. (*Life*, iii, 118 n.)
2 Gavin Hamilton (1730–1797), painter and excavator, who spent most of his life in Rome.
3 Pocket-book, September 11: "5, Mr. Agar." Sir Joshua was host at dinners on September 18 and 24.

Lord Spencer[1] tells me that he stood next, and was to have had them if your Grace had declined the purchase. One of the articles, he says, between Beyers and the Marquis was that he should bring the strangers as usual to see the copies, and which he says he is obliged to do, and, I suppose, swear they are originals; and it is very probable those copies will be sold again, and other copies put in their place. This trick has been played, to my knowledge, with pictures of Salvator Rosa by some of his descendants, who are now living at Rome, who pretend that the pictures have been in the family ever since their ancestor's death.[2]

The connoiseurs—or, rather, picture dealers, who are better judges of the prices of pictures—value the Sacriments at £5,000. Vandergnecht,[3] who is both a painter and dealer, says that if he had any idea of those pictures being to be sold, he would have sent out to Rome on purpose to purchase them. All these circumstances, I think, may

1 George John Spencer, Earl Spencer (1758–1834), famous for his library and art gallery. Sir Joshua was at this time painting his son, Lord Althorp.

2 Northcote, describing his lodgings at Rome in 1779, wrote: "These are rooms in the Palace of the late Queen of Sweden on the Trinita del Monte, near the Villa Medicis....This part in which I live Sir Joshua lived in some time when he was in Rome,...it is next door to the house of Salvator Rosa, and where his descendants still live". (Whitley's *Artists and their Friends in England*, ii, 313.)

3 Probably Vandergucht. *Cf. ante*, p. 158, n. 4.

help to make your Grace perfectly satisfied with your bargain.

Lord Mansfield's copy is quite finished, but, I am sorry and ashamed to say, the other of the children is not.[1] However, I am about it, and do every day a little to it. I hope within a fortnight to be able to send them both together. I cannot conclude this long and, I am afraid, tedious letter without again thanking your Grace for your last very kind and obliging letter....

CVIII[2]
To [JOSEPH HILL (?)]

Dear Sir   Oct. 10th 1786

I must acquaint you that having accepted a draught for six hundred Pounds for the Neptune which I bought at Rome,[3] which draught will be due in a few days, it will oblige me if you could discharge those Bills for mony which I have laid out for the Duke of Rutland.[4] It would still add

1 *Cf. ante*, p. 145, n. 1.
2 From a facsimile in the *Autograph Mirror* for April 7, 1866. The recipient may have been Joseph Hill, manager of Rutland's affairs in London, who was a friend of William Cowper and secretary to Lord Thurlow.   3 *Cf. ante*, p. 161.
4 In his account-book between the dates May, 1782, and September, 1785, is the following note:

"Duke of Rutland, debtor for
         Dutch pictures..........£ 247 15 2
         Paid duty..............   15 15 0

         Due from the Duke....... 263 10 2"

to the obligation if you can pay me the interest due on the Dukes Bonds which I hold. You may be sure I should not be sollicitous about this interest, if it was not for the reason I have mention'd, and now I would much rather endeavour to borrow it than put the Duke to the least inconvenience.

I am with great respect
Your most obedient servant

J REYNOLDS

CIX[1]

To JAMES BOSWELL

Wednesday [October 18, 1786.][2]

This being St. Lukes day, the Company of Painters dine in their Hall[3] in the City, to which

1 From the original in the possession of Rupert Colomb, Esq., now lent to the Royal Academy. First published in Cotton's *Gleanings*, 148.

2 Between 1760, when Boswell first came to London, and 1792, when Reynolds died, October 18 fell on a Wednesday four times only. On two of these occasions, 1775 and 1780, Boswell was in Scotland. The letter, therefore, must be dated either 1769 or 1786. I had selected the earlier year, but just as this book is about to be printed, have discovered with the aid of Mr W. T. Whitley an article in *The Morning Chronicle* for October 21, 1786, commenting on this festival and mentioning that the painters were "accompanied by Sir Joshua Reynold's, Mr. Boswell, and several of the Royal Academicians".

3 "Painter-Stainers Hall was in little Trinity Lane, on the South Side of Thames Street." (Quoted from Pennant by Cotton.) Sir Joshua was presented with the Freedom of the Company in 1784.

I am invited and desired to bring any friend with me.

As you love to see life in all its modes if you have a mind to go I will can[1] you about two o'clock, the black-guards dine at half an hour after

Yours

J REYNOLDS

CX[2]

To the DUKE OF RUTLAND

December 2, 1786.

...I did not receive your Grace's letter till to-day, though dated so far back as the 13th November, kept back by contrary winds; ten packets arrived at the same time. The picture has been finished some days and waits only for the frame, which the frame-maker says will require eight days longer. Mr. Burke gives me such an account of the young ladies that I dread the comparison of the originals with my copy.[3] Mr. Burke is very much pleased with his tour to Ireland, and speaks much of your Grace's great politeness to him. The voyage did not agree so well with his son;

1 "I will call on you" is crossed out and followed by "I will can you". The note was hastily written.
2 From *Rutland*, iii, 359 *et seq.*
3 *Cf. ante*, p. 145, n. 1. Burke had visited Ireland for a fortnight in October.

he was sea-sick in his passage over, and has continued ill ever since.

I sent to Mr. Hill[1] to enquire about the prints and books, which I find were sent away some time since. He supposes they are arrived by this time. I looked at the prints before they were packed up; I was mortified to see such trifling ornaments published with so much pomp, merely because they are antique or painted by some of Raffael's scholars in the Vatican. An indiscriminate admiration for everything that is antient appears to me full as prejudicial to the advancement of art as a total neglect of them would be.

Prince Rezzonico[2] was much mortified, he said, to see the Sacraments of Poussine in England, and for the same reason that you (speaking to me) may be glad; "But I must write to my brother," said he, "who is Secretary of State, that he should reprimand the inspectors for suffering those pictures to come out of Rome". Some time after this, Lady Spencer[3] told me that in consequence of this smuggling it is now death to attempt sending pictures out of Rome without being first examined....

1 *Cf. ante*, Letter cviii. The prints here discussed were mentioned in the last paragraph of Letter cvi.
2 Charles-Gaston, comte Rezzonico della Torre (1742–1796), man of letters, at this time travelling in England.
3 Lavinia Bingham (1762–1831), daughter of Lord and Lady Lucan, whose portrait by Sir Joshua had been exhibited this year.

CXI[1]

To JOHN BOYDELL

*Dec 8th 1786

Sir Joshua Reynolds presents his Comp^{ts}. to M^r. Alderman Boydell He finds in his Advertisement that he is styled Portrait Painter to his Majesty, it is a matter of no great consequence, but he does not know why his title is changed, he is styled in his Patent Principal Painter to His Majesty.

CXII[2]

To EDMOND MALONE

My dear Sir,   Dec. 15, 1786.

I wish you would just run your eye over my Discourse,[3] if you are not too much busied in what

1 From a facsimile in Graves and Cronin, facing p. 814. The original is in the possession of A. Edward Newton, Esq., of Philadelphia. The recipient (1719–1804), engraver, print-publisher, and (in 1790) Lord Mayor, had just issued proposals "to publish by subscription a most magnificent and accurate edition" of Shakespeare, edited by Steevens and illustrated by the prominent artists of the day. Sir Joshua, heading the list of artists, is termed "Portrait-Painter to his Majesty, and President of the Royal Academy". *Cf. post*, p. 174, n. 3.

2 From Cotton's *Notes*, 64. In 1912 the original was in the possession of the Messrs Maggs.

3 The thirteenth, delivered at the Royal Academy on December 11. Though the title-page is dated 1786, the *Discourse* was probably not published until the first week of the new year. *Cf. post*, Letter CXIV. Malone speaks of revising some of the *Discourses* in his memoir of Sir Joshua. *Works*, i, p. xliv.

you have made your own employment. I wish that you would do more than merely look at it,—that you would examine it with a *critical eye*, in regard to *grammatical correctness*, the propriety of expression, and the truth of the observations.

Yours,

J. REYNOLDS.

CXIII¹

To the Hon. CHARLES GREVILLE

*Dec. 23. 1786

Sir Joshua Reynolds presents his Comptˢ to Mʳ. Greville and begs leave to return his acknowledgements of the receipt of £157–10– for the Picture of Thais and his own Portrait

1 From the hitherto unpublished original in the possession of the Messrs Maggs. The recipient (1749–1809) was nephew of Sir William Hamilton. According to Fanny Burney, he had requested Sir Joshua to paint in the character of Thais a portrait of his mistress, whose name is given variously as Emily Pott, Emily Bertie, and Emily Coventry (*v.* Graves and Cronin, 162 *et seq.*, 1387). The portrait had been exhibited in 1781. The note is interesting when we learn that in October of this year Sir William Hamilton was worried about his nephew's financial condition (*v.* Whitley's *Artists and their Friends in England*, ii, 90).

CXIV[1]
To [HENRI JANSEN]

Dear Sir   London Jan 10th 1787

I have herewith sent the last Discourse, The Printing of which was delayed on account of the Christmas holydays when the Printers men will not work.

I should be much obliged to you for an Impression when the Translation[2] is finished

I am with great respect
Yours &c
J REYNOLDS

CXV[3]
To the DUKE OF RUTLAND

London, February 13, 1787.

...I will not trouble your Grace with the various causes of the pictures of the children[4] and

1 From the hitherto unpublished original in my possession. According to Sotheby's catalogue for a sale on December 13, 1918, the recipient was Strahan. Actually the letter was written to Henri, or Hendrik, Jansen (1741–1812), a Dutchman, who at this time was l'Inspecteur Général de l'Académie Royale de Musique in Paris. He is known chiefly for translating foreign works on art into French.

2 Jansen had written Sir Joshua in September, asking permission to translate the *Discourses* into French. *V.* Cotton's *Notes*, 64 *et seq.* The translation, which appeared in this year, also included Sir Joshua's notes on Mason's version of Dufresnoy's *Art of Painting*.

3 From *Rutland*, iii, 371 *et seq.*   4 *Cf. ante*, p. 145, n. 1.

172

London Jan 10ᵗʰ 1787

Dear Sir

I have herewith sent the last Discourse, The Printing of which was delayed on account of the Christmas holydays when the Printers men will not work.

I should be much obliged to you for an Impression when the Translation is finished

I am with great respect
Yours &c
J Reynolds

LETTER FROM REYNOLDS TO JANSEN
From a photograph of the original

of Lord Mansfield being delayed so long, it would take up the whole letter; I can only say they were inevitable; however, they are now on their way to Dublin. In regard to the Sacriments, I hear people continu[a]lly regret that they are not to remain in London; they speak on a general principle as wishing that the great works of art which this nation possesses are not (as in other nations) collected together in the capital, but dispersed about the country, and consequently not seen by foreigners, so as to impress them with an adequate idea of the riches in virtu which the nation contains. A thought is just come into my head that if your Grace is determined to send them to Belvoir, to let them stand in the Academy, in a room by themselves, during the Exhibition, to give an opportunity of their being seen by the students as well as the connoiseurs before they finally leave London. If your Grace has no objection to this scheme I am sure it would be of great service to the artists, both the young and the old.[1]

I have order'd very handsome frames to be made for them, at ten guineas each, and very broad, which I think gives a picture a more consequential air.

Mr. Lock's Discobolus,[2] as I have been informed,

1 *Cf. post*, Letter cxvii.
2 Mentioned in the tenth *Discourse*. (*Works*, ii, 21). William Locke (1732–1810), "whose knowledge and taste in the fine arts is universally celebrated", was the father of the amateur artist by the same name (1767–1847). *V*. Boswell's *Life*, iv, 43.

is not to be sold. At a sale which he had last year of his marbles and models, he bought that statue in; and I am told since that he intends to keep it for the use of his son, who is a youth of a most extraordinary genius in our art, and which his father intends he shall practice, tho he will have a very good fortune at his father's death.

I have, lately arrived, a modern statue of a Neptune with a Triton, which far exceeds Mr. Lock's statue, or any other in this nation. Your Grace may form some idea of it from the print in Rossi's Statues,[1] if such a book is to be found in Ireland. I bought it of Jenkins, who purchased all the statues in the Villa Negroni, formerly Villa Montalto; the subject is the *Quos ego* of Virgil.[2]

But the greatest news relating to virtu is Alderman Boydel's scheme of having pictures and prints taken from those pictures of the most interesting scenes of Shakespear[3], by which all the painters and engravers find engagements for eight or ten years; he wishes me to do eight pictures, but I have engaged only for one. He has insested on my taking earnest mony, and to my great surprise left upon my table five hundred pounds—to have as much more as I shall demand.

1 *Raccolta di Statue antiche e moderne*, published in 1704 by Domenico de Rossi, Roman engraver.
2 *Aeneid*, I, 135, where Neptune gazes on the storm.
3 *Cf. ante*, Letter CXI. Sir Joshua painted three of the series, "Puck", "Macbeth", and "The Death of Cardinal Beaufort".

I have enclosed Boydel's proposals and my last discourse, which I hope will meet with your Grace's approbation....

CXVI[1]

To LORD HARDWICKE
[1787.]

Sir Joshua Reynolds presents his Compliments to Lord Hardwick. Biondi an Italian who lives in Oxford Road on the right hand side of the way, not far from Orchard Street, his name on the door Sir Joshua has seen some Pictures which he has cleaned for the Duke of Rutland that were extremely well cleaned & mended better done than any he had ever seen before.

CXVII[2]

To the DUKE OF RUTLAND
London, May 3, 1787.

...I was very glad to find by your Grace's letter that you wished to have made some purchaces in Lord Northington's sale,[3] particularly portraits of Vandyck. Though I have not bought any

1 From the hitherto unpublished original in the British Museum (Add. MSS. 35,350, f. 51). On the MS. in pencil is written: "circ. 1783?". It seems more probable, however, that the letter was written between October 4, 1786 (*cf. ante*, p. 163), and October 24, 1787, when Rutland died.

2 From *Rutland*, iii, 386 *et seq.*

3 Robert Henley, second Earl of Northington (1747–1786), Rutland's predecessor as Lord Lieutenant of Ireland.

175

of those portraits, I have bought by far the most curious and most valuable part of that collection, which is a sketch upon board, in black and white, of the procession of Knights of the Garter. This sketch authenticates a circumstance that is always mentioned in Vandyck's life, of a project of King Charles of employing him totally on this subject to the exclusion of all other business, but that his demand of £80,000 being thought exorbitant, whilst they were treating for a less sum the King's troubles came on and put an end to the treaty. The sum demanded is incredible. I suspect, therefore, an o by some accident was added, which would bring it to £8,000, and even that would be, according to the value of mony at present, £24,000.

There were three or four portraits which were called Vandyck, but were certainly not of his hand. I did not think it worth while to send a commission for them. There was indeed a true picture of Claude Lorrain, but not his best, and had been much damaged.

The sketch[1] which I bought, with a view of offering it to your Grace at the price it cost me, whether much or little, was sold for sixty and some odd pounds. I sent a commission for a hundred. That your Grace may form some idea of it, I have spoilt a print by folding it in order to accompany this letter.

The King when I accompanyed him at the

1 Now in Belvoir Castle.

176

Exhibition[1] took much notice of the Poussins, more than I expected, as they are of a different kind from what he generally likes. He asked many questions—where they came from? out of what palace? what they cost? and whether there was any suspicion of their being copies? To all which questions I answered to the best of my knowledge.

I have been often angry with myself for having declined parting with the portrait of Albert Durer, as your Grace wished to have it in your collection. As it is a rare and curious thing, it cannot be better placed and fixed than at Belvoir; I shall therefore take the liberty of sending it with the Poussins.

I am extremely sorry to hear of her Grace's indisposition;[2] it may be hoped that the change of season may be as serviceable towards the establishment of her Grace's health as the change of climate to which she is so averse.

I am unwilling to give up all thought of going to Ireland this summer, but am in great doubt whether I shall be able to compass it. I am sure I am, as I ought to be, very much flattered by your Grace's kind invitation....

1 Pocket-book for April 27: "10, King".
2 A few weeks later her physicians told Sir Joshua that "the disorder on the nerves is wearing itself off by quiet hours, air, and exercise". (*Rutland*, iii, 391.)

CXVIII[1]

To JOSEPH BONOMI

July 2nd, 1787.

Sir Joshua Reynolds presents his compliments to Mr. Bonhomme, and is very sorry that his engagements have prevented him from calling on him since his misfortune.[2] He hopes to hear from himself that he is nearly recovered.

The business of this note is principally to desire that he would once more become a candidate to be an Associate of the Academy, when he hopes to be able to convince the Academicians of the propriety and even necessity of electing him an Associate, and consequently an Academician, &c.[3]

If he has not yet subscribed his name, he begs he would do it immediately, as the time for subscribing is nearly elapsed.[4]

---

1 From Leslie and Taylor, ii, 561 n. *et seq.* The recipient (1739–1808), an Italian architect, had lived in London since 1767.

2 "A broken arm, occasioned by the overturn of a carriage." (*Loc. cit.*)

3 Bonomi, who had been unsuccessful in his two attempts to be elected Associate, was Sir Joshua's candidate for Professor of Perspective in the Royal Academy, a position which could be held only by an Academician.

4 Candidates were required to post their names three months before the date of election, which in the present instance was December 3.

CXIX[1]

To BENNET LANGTON

Friday, August 31st, [1787.]

...*I have no children.* I therefore send the present, which I found on my return to town to *your* children.[2] It is scarce worth acceptance, and my only apology is that my friend thought it worth while to send them to me, I suppose therefore they are eminently good. I thought it necessary to be able to say I had tasted them, which makes a little deficiency in one of the pottles.[3]...

1 From Sotheby's catalogue for a sale July 6, 1910 (lot 62). The recipient (1737–1801), a member of the Club, had married in 1770. Between this date and Sir Joshua's death August 31 twice fell on a Friday, in 1781 and 1787. In 1781 Sir Joshua was travelling in the Low Countries; hence the date conjectured.
2 Langton had four sons and five daughters, who, according to Johnson, were "too much about him". (Boswell's *Life*, iii, 128.) Sir Joshua had just returned from a brief visit at Ampthill, the residence of the Earl of Upper Ossory.
3 *Cf.* Johnson's behaviour on receiving a jar of marmalade from Mrs Boswell. (*Life*, iii, 129 and note.)

CXX[1]

To GEORGE ROSE

Sir/   Royal Academy 14th Septr 1787

I have communicated your Letter to the Council of the Royal Academy in which we are orderd by the Lords Commissioners to insure the Appart^{nts} allotted to the Royal Academy. They beg leave to remark that there is no established Fund for the support of the Academy, and the proffits by which it is supported are altogether precarious, That such as they are, they are employed not for the benefit of the President & Council (who have no Sallaries) but for the Advancement of Art. That they consider the Building as the Kings House, not theirs, tho: His Majesty is so gracious as to permit them to make use of it; and therefore whether they can undertake from a Fund thus precarious, to insure one of the Kings Houses, is submitted to their Lordships, and if they are pleased to order them to make such insurance they shall certainly obey.

They beg leave to add that the little Fund which they have been able to accumulate, after defraying the Expences of the Academy, is appropriated to the relief of such Artists as are rendered incapable

1 From the hitherto unpublished copy in the minutes of the Council of the Royal Academy, under date of September 13. The recipient (1744–1818) was at this time one of the two secretaries in the office of the Treasury.

of following their Profession, or their distressed Families.

It is from these poor Artists therefore the Money must be taken, if the Insurance is insisted on by the Lords Commissioners.[1]

I am with the greatest respect
Your most Obedient humble Servt

JOSHUA REYNOLDS PRES^t

CXXI[2]

To BENNET LANGTON

Leicester fields [November] 23 [1787.][3]

Dear Sir

I am going this Evening to the Academy to propose M^r. Gibbon to be Professor of Antient History in the room of the late D^r. Franklin.[4]

There is another Professorship vacant Professor of Antient Litterature which was held by Dr Johnson.[5] If you have no objection to suceed our

1 The Lords Commissioners did insist upon this, and the Council submitted at the meeting held on December 31.
2 From the hitherto unpublished original in the possession of W. Westley Manning, Esq.
3 This corner of the letter is worn away in the MS. The correct month and year are determined by the fact that Gibbon and Langton were recommended at the meeting of the Council on November 23, 1787.
4 Thomas Francklin (1721–1784), Professor of Greek at Cambridge, had succeeded Goldsmith in this honorary position.
5 Langton had been selected for a similar position in Johnson's imaginary college. (Boswell's *Life*, v, 108.)

181

late friend I have no doubt but the Academy will accept my recommendation. There is no duty required, we desire only the honour of your name, for which you have the entrè of the Academy and we give you once a year a very good dinner, I mean that before the Exhibition and you see the Exhibition as often as you please *gratis*.

I have been writing in the dark and perceive now I have a candle that I have begun this letter on the wrong side.
                              Yours sincerely
                                        J REYNOLDS

CXXII[1]

To GEORGE BIRCH

Ap'l 22nd, 1788.

...I am so hurryed in preparing for the Exhibition that I have but just time to acknowledge the receipt of your obliging letter inclosing a draft for one hundred guineas being the first half-payment for Dr Ash's Picture[2] which Picture I hope to begin in two or three days and you may be

1 From catalogue 784, issued in 1923 by Henry Sotheran. The recipient was one of the governors of the General Hospital at Birmingham.
2 John Ash (1723–1798), physician, had organized the Eumelian Club (named after him), to which Sir Joshua belonged. He was one of the founders of the General Hospital at Birmingham, where the portrait here mentioned now hangs. The first sitting occurred April 28.

assured that no attention on my part shall be wanting in the finishing it.

I am with great respect,

Your most obedient servant,

JOSHUA REYNOLDS.

CXXIII[1]

To ANDREW STRAHAN

June 1, 1788.

... receivd a message from a family that I cannot refuse, of their intention of dining with me at Richmond this day....

I only beg you to believe that this does not proceed from a capricious disposition. I consider such engagements as I was under to-day, with you, in a much more serious manner than the generality of the world, and nothing but such circumstances as I am convinced would satisfy you, had I time to explain them, make me now break my engagement.[2]...

J REYNOLDS

1　The recipient's name, the date, and the second paragraph are from Sotheby's catalogue for a sale on May 23, 1897. Preceding the extract from the letter is the following statement: "Mentions that he is extremely mortified that he cannot see his correspondent to-day, as he is obliged to dine with some friends at Richmond". The first paragraph and signature are from the facsimile on p. 78 (Appendix) of Scott and Davey's *Guide to the Collector of Historical Documents, Literary MSS., and Autograph Letters*, London, 1891.

2　Pocket-book for this date: "5, Mr. Strahan".

CXXIV[1]

To CALEB WHITEFOORD

*Wednesday Nov 26 [1788]

If Mr Whitefoord is not engaged tomorrow Sir Joshua Reynolds requests the honor of his company at dinner five o'clock.

CXXV[2]

To EDMOND MALONE

Dear Sir   [December, 1788.]

You wont be *a zede*, signifies, you wont be *again said*, you will have your wicked will. In the other instance, *How a man a zed* is exactly what we

---

1 From the hitherto unpublished original in the British Museum (Add. MSS. 36,595, f. 208). Between 1769, when Sir Joshua was knighted, and 1792, when he died, November 27 fell on a Thursday three times, in 1777, 1783, and 1788. I have selected the latest of the three, since under that date Sir Joshua notes in his pocket-book that he is "at home" at five o'clock.

2 From a facsimile in the New York Public Library. In the memoir prefixed to Sir Joshua's *Works* (i, p. xliv) Malone writes: "Four of the latter Discourses...the author did me the honour to submit to my perusal....When he wrote his last Discourse, I was not in London". Possibly this letter accompanied the fourteenth *Discourse*, which had been delivered at the Royal Academy on December 10, 1788. *Cf. ante*, Letter CXII.

find in Shakespear and other old writers *You have said now.*[1]

The Exmoor Dialogue might be much better done if insteed of making an Z for an S the author had saught after the old language the old words which still exist or at least did exist when I was a boy, such as *daverd*, applied to a faded flower or a woman past her prime derived undoubtedly from cadavorosus, a word that Milton would have seized with greediness if it had occurred to him.

I have sent by your servant my Discourse which I shall take as a great favour if you not only will examine critically but will likewise add a little elegance

Yours sincerely

J REYNOLDS.

---

1 In 1771 was published anonymously the seventh edition of *An Exmoor Scolding...between two Sisters....also an Exmoor Courtship.* In this and subsequent editions there is a glossary, which explains most of the obscure words and phrases but does not include the two expressions which puzzled Malone. "Ya wont be a zed" occurs at the end of scene three of the *Courtship*; "How a man a zed" appears twice in the *Scolding*, once in each "bout". Sir Joshua refers to *Othello* (IV, ii, 204), where Iago says to Roderigo, "You have said now".

CXXVI[1]

To SIR WILLIAM CHAMBERS

*Feb 6th [1789?].

Sir Joshua Reynolds presents his Comp[ts]. to Sir Will[m] Chambers. He had company yesterday with him when he answerd his note co[n]cerning the Kings Picture. Sir William is, there is no doubt of his opinion that a formal application from a Company is necessary before this favour can be granted—an individual of that Company requesting to have the Kings Picture is certainly not sufficient.

CXXVII[2]

To GEORGE III

May it please Your Majesty   [March, 1789.]

Amidst the general joy dispersed through the whole Nation on the great and happy Event of the re-establishment of Your Majesty's health, May the President and Council, with the rest of the Academicians and Associates of the Royal Aca-

1 From the hitherto unpublished original in my possession. The letter was written some time after September, 1784, when Sir Joshua became Principal Painter to George III.
2 From the hitherto unpublished copy in the minutes of the Council for a meeting on March 19, 1789.

186

demy, be permitted humbly to offer their most sincere congratulations on this joyful occasion.[1]—

Impressed as we are with a due sense of the Blessings we enjoy in common with all other subjects, from the protection which Your Majesty has allways been pleas'd to extend to the Arts in general, and the peculiar Patronage which has been Graciously afforded to the Royal Academy in particular, We presume to hope for pardon for this intrusion.—

The Members of this Academy are truly sensible how much the prosperity and advancement of the Arts which they profess are connected with and dependant on, the health and welfare of their Royal Patron and Protector.

For the long continuance of Your Majesty's health, we offer up our most fervent prayers, and indulge our hopes, that those Arts which have been so successfully planted under Your Majesty's Royal Patronage may grow and flourish to their full maturity and perfection during a long and glorious Reign.—

1 The reference is to the King's recovery from a temporary attack of insanity. He had become delirious in November, was convalescing in February, and resumed his authority March 10. *Cf.* Leslie and Taylor, ii, 531.

CXXVIII[1]
To QUEEN CHARLOTTE

May it please Your Majesty.   [April, 1789.]

The President and Council with the rest of the Academicians and Associates of the Royal Academy, beg leave to present to Your Majesty their humble congratulations on the re-establishment of His Majesty's health.

The general joy which this great and auspicious event has diffus'd through every part of the Empire, is considerably augmented by reflecting on the happiness which that event has afforded to Your Majesty and the rest of the Royal Family, with whose grief, and with whose joy the whole Nation sympathize, and offer up their prayers that Your Majesty's reign may be long and prosperous, and never more be embitter'd by any Calamity.

1 From the minutes of the Council for a meeting held on April 6, 1789. At the preceding meeting, March 31, the President had been requested to write this letter.

CXXIX[1]

To RICHARD COSWAY

Dear Sir $\qquad$ April 22^{d}

If you will trust me with your sketch of Rubens of Jupiter & Venus, for a few days, I shall take it as a great favour

Yours sincerely

J REYNOLDS

CXXX[2]

To ROBERT LOVELL GWATKIN

Dear Sir $\qquad$ London August 20. 1789

I thank you for your kind information relating to my dear Ophy, I beg my love to her and to my sister,[3] not forgetting little Ophy,[4] If my sister is still with you, I wish you would send little Ophy

1 From the hitherto unpublished original recently sold by the Messrs Maggs. Not being able to date it, I have inserted it here because of the notable lack of letters written in 1789. The recipient, "Macaroni Miniature Painter" (1740–1821), was a native of Devonshire and a pupil of Hudson. His fine collection of pictures was sold in 1791.

2 From a copy of the hitherto unpublished original in the possession of R. G. Gwatkin, Esq. *Cf. ante*, Letter LV.

3 Mary Reynolds Palmer (1716–1794), the recipient's mother-in-law, who lived in Torrington. She was the author of *A Dialogue in the Devonshire Dialect.*

4 Theophila Gwatkin, the recipient's daughter, and the original of Sir Joshua's "Simplicity".

189

with her to Torrington and Mary[1] will bring her from thence to London where I hope we shall see you & Mrs Gwatkin next summer and then you may take her back if she wishes it and I can spare her.

I am forbid writing on account of my Eyes[2] so you must excuse the shortness of this Letter

Yours sincerely

J REYNOLDS

CXXXI[3]

To RICHARD BRINSLEY SHERIDAN

Dear Sir,— Leicester Fields, January 20, 1790.

I have, according to your orders, bespoke a very rich frame to be made for Mrs. Sheridan's picture. You will easily believe I have been often solicited to part with that picture and to fix a price on it, but to those solicitations I have always turned my deafest ear, well knowing that you would never give your consent, and without it I certainly should never part with it. I really value that picture at five hundred guineas. In the common course of business (exclusive of its being Mrs.

1 Mary Palmer, the recipient's sister-in-law.
2 On July 13 Sir Joshua had been compelled to abandon painting, owing to gutta serena, which had impaired his eyesight and was soon completely to deprive him of the use of his left eye.
3 From Leslie and Taylor, ii, 552 *et seq.* Mrs Sheridan's portrait ("St. Cecilia") had been painted in 1775. Leslie suggests that her husband had not heretofore claimed it because of his "impecuniosity".

Sheridan's picture) the price of a whole-length with two children would be three hundred; if therefore, from the consideration of your exclusive right to the picture, I charge one hundred and fifty guineas, I should hope you will think me a reasonable man. It is with great regret I part with the best picture I ever painted, for tho' I have every year hoped to paint better and better, and may truly say, *Nil actum reputans dum quid superesset agendum,*[1] it has not been always the case. However, there is now an end of the pursuit; the race is over whether it is won or lost.

I beg my most respectful compliments to Mrs. Sheridan.

I am, with the greatest respect,
Your most humble and
obedient servant,

JOSHUA REYNOLDS.

CXXXII[2]

To JOHN BACON

Dear Sir   [January, 1790.]

There is a report circulated by busy people, who interest themselves about what is going on in the Academy with which they have no business That you have declared your intention of giving

1 Lucan's *Pharsalia*, ii, 657.
2 From the hitherto unpublished original in my possession. The recipient (1740–1799) was the popular sculptor of the day.

your Vote for M^r. Edwards[1] whether he produces a drawing or not. This report I have treated with the contempt such a Calumny deserves, that neither yourself M^r. Hodges[2] nor any of the rest of the Council were capable of such duplicity of conduct I repeated to my informer, the Letter which was sent to M^r. Edwards That it was the *unanimous* opinion of the Council that he could not be a candidate unless &c.[3]

The Gentleman still persevering in his opinion. I beg you would give the means of confuting him under your own hand

         I am with great respec[t]

Yours

J REYNOLDS

1 Edward Edwards (1738–1806), now chiefly known for his continuation of Walpole's *Anecdotes of Painters*, was a candidate for the professorship of perspective, but had refused to submit one of his drawings to the Academy as a specimen of his abilities. Sir Joshua opposed him, favouring Bonomi (*cf. ante*, Letter CXVIII). An account of the resulting rupture is given in Leslie and Taylor, ii, 553–585.

2 William Hodges (1744–1797), landscape-painter.

3 In an unpublished part of his account of the quarrel with the Academy (now in the Academy's possession) Sir Joshua wrote: "About three months before the Election the Council in answer to a Letter receiv'd from Mr. Edwards in which he *demanded* the liberty of giving a lecture to the Academy as his Specimen to shew how well he was qualified to be Professor, informed him that he 'could not be consider'd as a Candidate to be an Acadⁿ in order to be Profess of Perspective unless he produced a Drawing', and added that the Election would be on the 10th of Feb."

CXXXIII[1]

To JOSEPH BONOMI

Dear Sir, Leicester Fields, Feby. 11, 1790.

I am sorry for the ill-success we have met with in our business[2] and that I have been the cause of giving you so much trouble needlessly. I can only say I did not think it possible, to have made such a combination against merit, but what can stand against perseverance? I suppose you may have been apprised that this infamous Cabal was begun when you was first proposed as a Candidate[3] and has been encreasing ever since.

However, I may flatter myself in my vain moments that my leaving the Academy at this time may be some detriment to it. I cannot persuade myself any longer to rank with such beings, and have therefore this morning ordered my name to be erased from the list of Academicians.

I should be glad to have in my house for a few

1 From an article in *The Times Literary Supplement*, July 15, 1920 (xix, 456), written by Col. J. I. Bonomi, a descendant of the recipient. The letter was partly printed by Leslie and Taylor (ii, 575 n.).
2 His failure to be elected an Academician at the General Meeting held the day before made him ineligible to be made Professor of Perspective.
3 In the spring of 1786.

To JOSEPH BONOMI   [*1790*

days those two drawings¹ or one of them when it is convenient for you to spare it as a full vindication to my friends of the merit which I recomended.

Yours sincerely,

J. REYNOLDS.

CXXXIV²

To SIR WILLIAM CHAMBERS

Sir,   [February, 1790.]

I find that the causes of my resigning the Presidency of the Royal Academy, have been grossly, & as I conceive from very unjustifiable motives, misrepresented. I am indifferent about the opinion of such people as I know to be as injudicious as the spreaders of the Reports are malicious. But I should be deeply concerned, if my Sovereign, the Patron of the Academy under whose auspicious Patronage it has so long flourished could be prevailed on to conceive me for one moment or in one instance insensible to the gracious

1 "The largest is of a saloon in the house of Mrs. Montagu in Portman Square, and the other is the library at Lansdowne House." (Leslie and Taylor, ii, 572 n.)

2 From a rough draft in Sir Joshua's hand, now in the possession of the Royal Academy. First partly published by Leslie and Taylor (ii, 578 *et seq.*). The recipient (1726–1796), chiefly responsible for the foundation of the Academy, was its first treasurer.

194

and condescending message which his Majesty has been pleased to send through you. I received it with the most profound respect and the warmest gratitude, as a consolation of my retreat & the greatest honour of my life. His Majesty by expressing his desire for my continuance has born a testimony to my good intentions for his service as President of his Academy. This is a full and final sentence on the representations of those who described me as capable of abusing a very small portion of Authority, in comparatively small concerns in order to gratify my own irregular & feeble passions. Lay me most humbly at his Majesty's feet, and assure his Majesty that in quitting the Presidency of the Royal Academy I felt the most sensible pain and that nothing could remove me from it but the certainty that it was absolutely impossible for me to perform my duty any longer.

I thought that the Professors Chairs ought to be filled by Persons skilful in the branch of Art which they professed and by those only and not by men less skilful in the particular branch though otherwise of high merit With all my self partiality I should have given a decided negative to any proposition which should be made for appointing me to the Professorship, of Anatomy or Perspective. But of one thing I am sure that a specimen of an Artists performance as a tittle to the Academick place and office he is Candidate for ought not to be refuced Admission Where such a precedent is established I cannot be any longer of use in that Academy.

The Academy thought differently from me and probably on better grounds I submitted to their judgment and I resigned. I am confident that his Majesty, a sovereign equally distinguished for his Justice and his Benevolence will graciously condescend to receive the humble apology of any Person whose conduct is in question and who has the most inconsiderable relation to his service, and who has been all his life, and will be for what remains of it most dutifully sensible of all the distinctions and honours received from his Majestys goodness

I have the honour to be

J. REYNOLDS.

CXXXV[1]

To SIR WILLIAM CHAMBERS

Dear Sir   [February, 1790.]

I send you a letter which I had just written before you returned my last. I wrote that letter, which I now enclose[2] because I wished to express with more clearness, my motives for declining the

1 From a rough draft in Sir Joshua's hand, now in the possession of the Royal Academy. First published by Leslie and Taylor (ii, 580 *et seq.*).

2 Letter CXXXIV in this collection.

Presidency. I request that you will do me the justice to lay it before his Majesty. Hitherto our correspondence related to the Presidency only your last letter to me conveys your desire that though I have been driven from the Chair of President I may still continue a member of the Academy. If I could be of no service as President, as you know I could not, I am yet to learn what service I can do in the character of a simple Academician. That Character too will be rendered still more ineffectual by the little attention paid to my wishes for the honour of the Academy, when I was in a situation of more importance you think it a sacrifice due to the Kings condescension & to my own character that it will please his Majesty obviate conclusions and aspersions which might prove disagreeable to me; the only one of these motives which could have any weight with me, is your opinion that it would please his Majesty. But if I think myself in honour and conscience obliged with all gratitude & humility, to decline the honour of Presidency when His Majesty has most graciously condescended to desire I would continue in it, I beg you to consider what reasons I can have for continuing a private member of [it;][1] in my opinion it must give his Majesty and the world a poor notion of my discretion and of my zeal for his service in my humble walk; that it will be a sacrifice to my Character is extraordinary

1 Left blank in MS.

indeed. what my Character in any light will gain
by declining the honours of the Academy and continuing in a subordinate station, you best understand   I do not, if you mean by character, my
moral character I hope it stands in no need of
sacrifices. "That it will obviate aspersions" I must
to satisfy you upon this point beg leave to remind
you of what you have said, "that you have known
me for forty years". in that time you may have
known (or you ought not to have continued my
acquaintance so long) that I am in a state of reputation [to defy] unfounded aspersions and if I had
no other reason for quiting the Academy than to
prove to you and those who may join with you in
this kind of threat, that I am not to be moved with
fear of those aspersions I would instantly resign
if I had not before resolved on it That this sacrifice
will obviate conclusions which might prove disagreeable to me, cannot have much more weight
upon my mind, if the natural conclusion be drawn
it will be this, that I do not approve of the method
of chusing members of the Academy to places in
it, without the fair mode of competition, that I did
not like the method of turning out with scorn &
every mark of personal ill will & ill manners to
myself, works that are the [titles]¹ of the Candidate
to the place he sollicits, and which did honour to
the Academy. If this conclusion be drawn it is a
conclusion to which I can have no objection. It is

1 Left blank in MS.

198

the only conclusion I would have drawn from my retreat. I do not wish to remain in the Academy to countenance a direct opposite conclution, which is that my resignation of the Presidency was, as you are pleased to think this my present resignation from motives disrespectful to the Patron and re-vengeful to the members of the Academy when in reality it was done on account of your departure from the most essential rules of the Academy, with-out the observance of which the choice to officers in the Academy & to the Rank of Academicians itself must in future become a matter of party and Cabal and not of open & honourable competition.

I have the honour to be with great respect
your most humble obedient &c

J REYNOLDS

CXXXVI[1]

To JOHN RICHARDS

Sir   Leicester Fields Feb[y] 22[d],: 1790

I beg you would inform the Council, which I understand meet this Evening, with my fixed resolution of resigning the Presidency of the Royal

1 From the minutes of the Council of the Royal Academy for a meeting held February 23. First published by Northcote, ii, 252. This was the second of two letters of resignation. The first one, written February 11 (*cf. ante*, Letter CXXXIII) "from the in-temperate language of it, he was persuaded to withdraw, and

199

Academy, and consequently my seat as Academician. As I can be no longer of any service to
the Academy as President, it would be still less in
my power, in a subordinate station; I therefore
now take my final leave of the Academy with my
sincere good wishes for its prosperity, and with all
due respect to its members

I am

Sir

Your most humble and most obedient
Servant,

JOSHUA REYNOLDS

P.S. Sir W^m. Chambers has two Letters of mine,[1]
either of which, or both he is at full liberty to communicate to the Council.

another to the same effect, but written in terms that approached
somewhat nearer to moderation, was substituted in its stead ".
(Gwynn's *Northcote*, 213.) The recipient (*d.* 1810) had been
Secretary of the Academy since 1788.

1 Letters CXXXIV and CXXXV in this collection. After three weeks
of confusion Sir Joshua was persuaded to withdraw his resignation, and resumed his position as President March 16.

CXXXVII[1]

To the Right Reverend THOMAS PERCY

My Lord,   Leicester Fields, March 13, 1790.

I have put the little business that you intrusted me with into the hands of Mr. Boswell, who, indeed, desired it, as he said he owed your Lordship a letter.

I write or read as little as possible on account of my eyes, and *this* letter is only to ward off the appearance of inattention till I shall have the honour of seeing your Lordship, which we are all glad to hear will be soon.

I am, with the greatest respect,

J. REYNOLDS.

CXXXVIII[2]

To BENJAMIN WEST

April 8th [1790].[3]

Sir Joshua Reynolds presents his Compliments to M[r]. West. He has receiv'd an Invitation from

1 From Nichols's *Illustrations of...Literary History*, viii, London, 1858, 277. Percy had asked Sir Joshua to send him Burke's speech on the French Revolution. *V. Letters of James Boswell*, ed. Tinker, Oxford, 1924, 391.

2 From the original, which in November, 1925, was in the possession of Thomas Madigan, Esq. First published in Arnold's *Ventures in Book Collecting*, New York, 1923, 139. On the reverse of the original there is a sketch made by West.

3 This year is given in Sotheby's catalogue for a sale held on February 23, 1909.

To BENJAMIN WEST   [*1790*

M^r. Hankey¹ to come & see his Drawings on Wednesday next. This morning he has received the inclosed Letter from M^r. Hankey. If M^r. West accepts of the invitation, Sir Joshua will send his Coach to M^r. West's house at half an hour after one o'clock and accompany him there.

CXXXIX²

To MRS. THEOPHILA PALMER GWATKIN

My Dear Niece   London April 15 1790

Tho, as you very well know, I am but a bad Correspondent yet I would not neglect answering your Letter, It would be superfluous to tell you that we should be glad to see you, and it was with great pleasure I read the Post-script which informs me that little Offy comes with you I write as little as I can, so adieu—my Comp^{ts} to M^r. Gwatkin

Yours most affectionately

J REYNOLDS

1 Thomas Hankey, banker, had inherited from his uncle, John Barnard, a valuable collection of prints and drawings. (*The Farington Diary*, v, London, 1925, 221 *et seq.*) It was doubtless this collection which Sir Joshua and West were to examine.
2 From the hitherto unpublished original in the John Rylands Library, Manchester.

CXL¹

To JAMES NORTHCOTE

[May, 1790.]

Sir Joshua Reynolds requests the honor of Mʳ Northcote['s] company at dinner next Monday the 24 of May 5 o'clock

CXLI²

To JOSIAH WEDGWOOD

*May 24ᵗʰ [1790.]

Sir Joshua Reynolds having been informed by Baron ——³ that Mʳ Wedgwood was seeking for a medal of the King of Hungary, has taken the liberty of sending the inclosed which he received from him when he was Grand Duke of Tuscany, and hopes it will answer his purpose.⁴

1 From a copy of the hitherto unpublished original in the possession of M. H. Spielmann, Esq. "1790", which appears at the lower right-hand corner of the note, is undoubtedly Northcote's addition.

2 From a copy of the original in the possession of James S. Maher, Esq., of Garrison, N.Y. First published in the *Catalogue of Literary Treasures of the late Gen. Brayton Ives* (Amer. Art Galleries, April 8, 1915, lot 804). The recipient (1730–1795), famous potter, has given the year in his endorsement.

3 Blank in MS.

4 Leopold II, who had succeeded his brother as Emperor on February 20 had sent Sir Joshua the medal in 1776. *Cf. ante*, Letter xxxv. Without doubt it served as a model for the many cameos which Wedgwood sent to Frankfurt in this year. *V.* Barnard's *Chats on Wedgwood Ware*, London, 1924, 185 *et seq.*

CXLII[1]

To JOHN WILKES

*Leicester Fields [June 4, 1790.][2]

Sir Joshua Reynolds presents his Comp[ts] to M[r]. Wilkes and returns him many thanks for the present he has made him, the value of which is much encreased in his estimation by the honour of receiving them from him[3]

He is very much flatterd by M[r]. Wilkes' polite attention to him.

1 From the original in the Gratz Collection, in the possession of the Pennsylvania Historical Society. First published in *The Correspondence of the late John Wilkes...*, iv, London, 1805, 235. The recipient (1727–1797), famous politician, had known Sir Joshua for more than forty years. *V. ante*, Letter IV.

2 The letter is undated. Nichols (*Literary Anecdotes of the Eighteenth Century*, ix, London, 1815, 470) dates it June 4 and prints it together with a number of similar notes of thanks which were written in 1790.

3 Wilkes had sent him a copy of his edition of Theophrastus, which had been printed in this year solely for presentation to his friends. (Nichols, *op. cit.* 68, 468 *et seq.*)

CXLIII[1]

To CATHERINE II

[August 6 (?), 1790.][2]

The approbation which your Imperial Majesty has been graciously pleased to express of the Academical Discourses which I presumed to lay at your Majestys feet, I truly consider as the great honour of my Life, That condescending acceptance of my attempts raises me in my own estimation & must of course advance my reputation in the Eyes of my Country men. Your Imperial Majesty has left nothing undone to give all possible lustre to this most gracious mark of your protection by the magnificent present which encloses it.[3] This

1 From a copy of the hitherto unpublished original made on September 14, 1790, by Mary Palmer in a letter to her cousin, William Johnson. The recipient (1729–1796), Empress of Russia, had commissioned Sir Joshua to paint for her his "Infant Hercules".

2 The letter was written after March 5 (v. Northcote, ii, 217) and before August 17, when Mary Palmer mentions it in a letter to her cousin. Opposite August 6 in the pocket-book Sir Joshua has written: "note re Hercules", which may refer to this letter.

3 She had received with the "Infant Hercules" the 1778 edition of the *Discourses*, accompanied by Jansen's translation (v. *ante*, Letter CXIV), and in return had sent Sir Joshua "a gold snuff-box, adorned with her profile in *bas relief*, set in diamonds... containing what is infinitely more valuable, a slip of paper, on which are written with her Imperial Majesty's own hand, the following words: '*Pour le Chevalier Reynolds en témoignage du contentement que j'ai ressentie à la lecture de ses excellens discours sur la peinture*'". (Boswell's *Life*, iii, 370.)

I shall carry about me as my title to distinction &
which I can never produce but with a sight of that
August Personage who whilst by her wise government she contributed to the happiness of a great
portion of mankind under her dominion, is pleased
to extend her favorable influence, to whatever
may decorate Life in any part of the World, that
whilst I endeavour to demonstrate my gratitude
for the distinction I have received I may have
further motives to such gratitude by receiving
accessions to my reputation, & that Posterity may
know (since now I may indulge the hope that I
may be known to Posterity) that your Imperial
Majesty has design'd to permit me to sollicit the
patronage of a Soveriegn to whom all the Poets,
Philosophers, & Artists of the time have done
homage & whose approbation has been courted by
all the Geniuses of her Age. With every sentiment
of profound veneration and attachment I am your
Majestys most humble & most devoted Servant

                                        J REYNOLDS.

CXLIV¹

To [the DUKE OF LEEDS]

My Lord   Leicester fields Oct. 4 1790

I may say, without much affectation of modesty that the Picture which I have the honour of sending by the bearer, is, either as a subject, or as a Picture scarce worth hanging² however it is very flattering to me that Your Grace is of another opinion, and your being so, I seriously consider as the greatest honour of my life

I am with the greatest respect

Your Graces most humble
and most obedient servant

JOSHUA REYNOLDS

1 From the hitherto unpublished original in possession of the Messrs Maggs. The recipient was probably Francis Osborne, fifth Duke of Leeds (1751–1799), a member of the Club and the Society of Dilettanti, and later a pall-bearer at Sir Joshua's funeral.

2 "The last portrait which he painted of himself, (with spectacles,) in 1788, is extremely like him, and exhibits him exactly as he appeared in his latter days, in domestick life. It is a three-quarters, in the collection of the Earl of Inchiquin; and his Grace the Duke of Leeds has a duplicate of it." (*Works*, i, p. lxxvii, n. 45.) It is undoubtedly this copy that Sir Joshua here refers to. The recipient has endorsed the letter: "Sir Joshua Reynolds, with His Picture".

CXLV[1]

To LADY OSSORY

Madam,— London, January 1, 1791.

I am just setting out for Beaconsfield,[2] with an intention to stay there all next week, which, I am sorry to say, will prevent me from waiting on your Ladyship at Ampthill:—I should have said, throwing myself at your Ladyship's feet, and expressing my thanks and acknowledgments for the honour conferred on me by this new mark of favour.

I really think, as it is the work of your Ladyship's own hand, it is too good to wear. I believe I had better put it up with the letter which accompanied it, and show it occasionally, as I do the Empress of Russia's box and letter of her own handwriting. I will promise this at least, that when I do *ware* it, I will not take a pinch of snuff that day—I mean, after I have it on.[3]

Such a rough beast[4] with such a delicate waistcoat.—I am sorry to say I am forced to end

1 From Leslie and Taylor, ii, 596. The original is in the possession of W. Westley Manning, Esq. For the recipient *v. ante*, Letter L.
2 To visit Burke.
3 She had sent him a tambour-worked waistcoat of her own embroidering. "What a quantity of snuff Sir Joshua took! I once saw him at an Academy-dinner, when his waistcoat was absolutely powdered with it." (Rogers's *Table-Talk*, London, 1856, 21.)
4 Taylor suggests "breast".

abruptly, as the coach is waiting. Miss Palmer
desires her most respectful compliments, and I beg
mine to Lord Ossory and the ladies.

I am, with the greatest respect,

Your Ladyship's, &c. &c.,

J. REYNOLDS.

CXLVI[1]

To LADY OSSORY

Madam,—   Beaconsfield, January 3, 1791.

Your eloquence is irresistible. I am resolved to
set out next Monday, and call on my way at
Woburn Abbey,[2] and from thence gladly accept
of your Ladyship's kind offer of a conveyance to
Ampthill.

Perhaps, if I was cunning, I should throw some
difficulties in the way, and by that means procure
more flattering letters, and more good verses.[3] But
I have heard say that too much cunning destroys
its own purpose; and I fear that my coyness in the
present case would make you all so angry, that you
would never more invite me, or think me worth
saying a civil thing to, which would break my
heart.

1 From Leslie and Taylor, ii, 597.
2 The seat of the Duke of Bedford.
3 She had enclosed with her invitation a copy of Col. Fitzpatrick's
prologue to a play which was to be acted at Ampthill.

My apprehension at present is, that when I come I shall not be able to hear a word. Young timid actors are not apt to throw their voices out sufficient for a deaf man; however, I have an eye, which will be sufficiently gratified if beauty and elegance, if—I believe I had better reserve what I have further to say on this inexhaustible subject till I come to Ampthill.

I am, with the greatest respect,

Your Ladyship's

Most humble and most obedient

servant,

J. REYNOLDS.

CXLVII[1]

To [EDMOND MALONE]

My Dear Sir   London March 8th 1791

In requires some apology to expect you to distribute the enclosed Books,[2]—I believe the persons to whom they are directed are all your friends— I am sorry to hear Lord Charlemont[3] has been un-

1 From the original in the Malone Collection at the Bodleian Library (Bodl. MS. Malone 26, f. 147). First published in Cotton's *Notes*, 73.
2 Probably copies of the fifteenth *Discourse*, which had been delivered on December 10 of the preceding year and had recently been published. (*Cf. Letters of James Boswell*, ed. Tinker, Oxford, 1924, 429.)
3 James Caulfeild, fourth Viscount, afterwards first Earl, of Charlemont (1728–1799), who was a member of the Club.

well, which gives real concern to all that know him, I am afraid to express my particular esteem and affection as it would have an air of impertinent familiarity and equality. and for another reason shall say nothing regarding yourself for fear of the suspicion of being a Toad-eater, a character for which we Gentlemen about town, have great abhorrence and are apt to run too much on the other side in order to avoid it, however I will venture to say thus much, that you are every day found wanting and wished for back, and by no-body more than your very sincere friend and humble servant

J.REYNOLDS

Today is Shrove Tuesday, and no Johnson.¹
I beg my most respectfull comp^{ts}. Lord Sunderlin.²

CXLVIII³
To SIR JOSEPH BANKS

Dear Sir   March 15 1791

I shall be obliged to you if you would summons the Committee to meet any day that is most con-venient to yourself, in order finally to determine

1 *The Life of Johnson*, which Boswell had hoped to publish on that day. *V. Letters of James Boswell*, 410, 414, 424, 427.
2 Richard Malone, Baron Sunderlin (1738–1816), the recipient's brother.
3 From the original in my possession. A facsimile faces p. 250 in vol. v of the *Catalogue of the Collection of Autograph Letters...formed...by Alfred Morrison*, 1891.

about D^r. Johnsons Monument^I I should think the morning—about two o'clock would be the best time, From the number of engagements that every man has, it can scarce be expected we can meet to a dinner

I am with great respect

Yours &c

J REYNOLDS

CXLIX²

To the Right Hon. LORD HERVEY

My Lord,   London, March 19, 1791.

Though I have not the honour of being known to your lordship, yet I trust I shall be excused in the liberty I take of recommending to your lordship's patronage and protection the bearer of this— Mr. Howard, a young painter who is on his way to Rome.³ He gained the first prize of our

---

1 On January 5, 1790, a meeting of the friends of Dr Johnson was held to determine upon a suitable monument to his memory. Banks presided. The committee elected was made up of Banks, Windham, Burke, Malone, Metcalfe, Boswell, and the two surviving executors, Sir William Scott and Sir Joshua. *V. Gentleman's Magazine* for January, 1790, lx, i, 3.

2 From Northcote, ii, 273. John Augustus Hervey, Lord Hervey (1757-1796), was ambassador at Florence from 1787 to 1794.

3 Henry Howard (1769-1847), painter of portraits and historical pictures. He won the prize with his "Caractacus recognising the Dead Body of his Son", a subject taken from Mason's *Caractacus.*

Academy in December last, and I had the pleasure of telling him, when I delivered the gold medal, that it was the opinion of the academicians that his picture was the best that had been presented to the academy ever since its establishment.

To such merit I rest assured that an introduction alone is sufficient to procure your lordship's favour.

I am with the greatest respect,

    Your Lordship's

        Most humble and most obedient servant,

            JOSHUA REYNOLDS.

CL[1]

To JAMES NORTHCOTE

Dear Sir,—   March 26, 1791.

Mr. Desanfans[2] told me yesterday a most extraordinary story, that the Lord Mayor[3] should say to me that he had an intention of introducing whole-length portraits of Lord Mayors into the Mansion House, and that he added he intended to

---

1 From Gwynn's *Northcote*, 228, which derives from a copy of the original made by the recipient. First published by Leslie and Taylor (ii, 599).

2 Noel Joseph Desenfans (1745–1807), picture-dealer.

3 John Boydell. *V. ante*, Letter CXI.

employ Northcote and Opie,¹ and that I advised him not to employ them but Mr. Lawrence.²

The reason of my mentioning this to you is in hopes that you will help me in endeavouring to trace this story to its fountain-head.

If my opinion is considered as of any value, it is certainly your interests to detect this mischief-maker; I am far from thinking that the Lord Mayor is the author.

I am, &c.,

Yours sincerely,

J. REYNOLDS.

CLI³

To EDMOND MALONE

Dear Sir,—   Leicester Fields, April 9, 1791.

Boswell has been just sealing a letter to you. I begged before the wafer was dry that he would insert a paragraph; he says there is not room for a single word. All that I wanted was to beg you would get as many subscriptions as you can ex-

---

1 John Opie (1761–1807), portrait and historical painter.
2 Sir Joshua was greatly impressed with young Thomas Lawrence. *Cf. London Chronicle* for November 2–4, 1790, lxviii, 438. From this fact and from Northcote's story it seems obvious that Sir Joshua actually made this remark and is here merely extricating himself from an embarrassing situation.
3 From Leslie and Taylor, ii, 603. The original is in the possession of R. B. Adam, Esq. It is addressed: "Edmond Malone, Esq.,/Sackville Street, Dublin".

clusive of the Club, such as the Chancellor,[1] Secretary Hutchinson,[2] &c. As the Monument (to Dr. Johnson) is to be in St. Paul's, and the figure colossal, it will require £1200. Of this sum we can count only upon £900. The rest I have engaged to give myself if it cannot be provided from others.

I have received a bill of lading for the two hogsheads of claret.[3]

Yours sincerely,

J. REYNOLDS.

CLII[4]

To WILLIAM CRIBB

Dear Sir,   14 April 1791.

Go to my House & tell George to deliver to you a picture which hangs over the chimney in

1 John Fitzgibbon, Lord Fitzgibbon, later Earl of Clare (1749–1802).

2 John Hely-Hutchinson (1724–1794), Secretary of State in Ireland, and a close friend of Burke.

3 According to Leslie, a present to the Club. *Cf. Letters of James Boswell*, 423.

4 From a copy of the hitherto unpublished original, made in 1847 by J. H. Anderdon, and inserted in vol. 2 of his copy of Edwards's *Anecdotes of Painters*, which is now in the Print Room of the British Museum. The existence of these interesting volumes was brought to my notice by Mr W. T. Whitley. The recipient was Sir Joshua's frame-maker.

The letter is explained by an article in Willis's *Current Notes* for September, 1857. Sir Joshua, irritated by Desenfans, the picture-dealer, who constantly praised the old masters and sneered at the moderns, had his former pupil Marchi copy

215

the blue chamber and get it lined & varnishd which it very much needs, as it has not been moved for 30 years.[1] It is a Copy after Claude, if it were original it would be worth a thousand guineas, and as a copy I should think it worth half, at any rate I will not sell it under 200 g^s if you cannot sell it at that price let the handsome frame it has be new gilt, and let it be hung up in the parlour by the time I come to town.[2]

Yours sincerely

J REYNOLDS.[3]

P.S. Do not let anybody know to whom the picture belongs.

Claude's "View near the Castle of Gondolfo". The copy was then dried, smoked, and substituted for the original in the frame over the fire-place in the dining-parlour. This letter was then sent to Cribb, who was in the secret, and who "accidentally" allowed it to be seen by Desenfans. The dealer at once fell into the trap, paying £200 for Marchi's copy. Sir Joshua, returning the draft, expressed surprise that a man of such discrimination had been deceived by the work of a modern.

1 He had moved into his house at Leicester Fields thirty-one years previously.

2 He attended meetings of the Council on April 11 and 18, which would seem to give the recipient scant time in which to work. Apparently he was living at his house at Richmond (*v*. Leslie and Taylor, ii, 606).

3 According to Sotheby's catalogue for a sale held July 25, 1905 (lot 620), Sir Joshua "has himself obliterated his signature".

CLIII[1]

To THOMAS CADELL

April 18 1791

Sir Joshua Reynolds presents his Comp[ts]. to M[r]. Cadell. and begs leave to acquaint him that the Committee for D[r]. Johnsons Monument returns their thanks to him and the rest of the subscribers for the liberal benefaction of one hundred pounds which sum if M[r]. Cadel will please to pay to the bearer (his servant Ralph Kirkley) Sir Joshua will transmit it to M[r]. Metcalf[2] the Treasurer

CLIV[3]

To WILLIAM GILPIN

Dear Sir,   London, April 19th, 1791.

Tho I read now but little, yet I have read with great attention the essay, which you was so good to put into my hands, on the difference between the *beautiful*, and the *picturesque*; and I may truly

1 From a photostat of the hitherto unpublished original in the possession of the Johnson Society, Lichfield. The recipient (1742–1802) was printer to the Royal Academy.

2 Philip Metcalfe, M.P. (1722–1818), who had accompanied Sir Joshua on his trip to Flanders in 1781, and who acted as one of his executors.

3 From Gilpin's *Three Essays: on Picturesque Beauty; on Picturesque Travel; and on Sketching Landscape* . . ., London, 1792, 34 *et seq.* The recipient (1724–1804) was the author of a number of biographies and books on art.

217

say, I have received from it much pleasure, and improvement.

Without opposing any of your sentiments, it has suggested an idea, that may be worth consideration—whether the epithet *picturesque* is not applicable to the excellences of the inferior schools, rather than to the higher. The works of Michael Angelo, Raphael, &c. appear to me to have nothing of it; whereas Reubens, and the Venetian painters may almost be said to have nothing else.

Perhaps *picturesque* is somewhat synonymous to the word *taste*; which we should think improperly applied to Homer, or Milton, but very well to Pope, or Prior. I suspect that the application of these words are to excellences of an inferior order; and which are incompatible with the grand stile.

You are certainly right in saying, that variety of tints and forms is picturesque; but it must be remembred, on the other hand, that the reverse of this—(uniformity of colour, and a long continuation of lines,) produces grandeur.

I had an intention of pointing out the passages, that particularly struck me; but I was afraid to use my eyes so much.

The essay has lain upon my table; and I think no day has passed without my looking at it, reading a little at a time. Whatever objections presented themselves at first view,[1] were done away on a

1 "Sir Joshua Reynolds had seen this essay, several years ago, through Mr. Mason, who shewed it to him. He then made some

closer inspection: and I am not quite sure, but that is the case in regard to the observation, which I have ventured to make on the word *picturesque*.

I am, &c.

JOSHUA REYNOLDS.

CLV[1]

To [THOMAS CADELL]

April 20, [1791.]

...Pray send me two volumes of the Discourses unbound....

objections to it: particularly he thought, that the term *picturesque*, should be applied only to the *works of nature*." (Gilpin, *op. cit.* 35 n.) *Cf.* Leslie and Taylor, ii, 606 *et seq.* "Picturesque" is not in Johnson's *Dictionary*.

1 From catalogue 320, issued in 1918 by the Messrs Maggs. The letter is there dated "ca. 1792". Since Sir Joshua was not living on April 20, 1792, I have assumed that the letter was written the previous year, when his last *Discourse* (the fifteenth) was published. The recipient was probably the printer to the Royal Academy.

CLVI[1]

To GEORGE ROSE

Sir   Royal Academy Apr: 20, 1791

The Council of the Royal Academy beg leave to express their wish that the report of the Architects appointed to survey the Buildings erected in Somerset Place could be made public previous to the opening of the Exhibition.[2] If there should be no impropriety in the request they flatter themselves that the Lords Commissioners of His Majesty's Treasury will enable them to give to the public this information.

I have the honour to be
Sir Your most humble
and most obedient Servant

JOSHUA REYNOLDS, PRES[t]:

1 From the hitherto unpublished copy in the minutes of the Council for a meeting held April 26, 1791.
2 One of the beams which supported the floor of the Academy had given way while Sir Joshua was delivering his last *Discourse*, December 10, 1790. A committee of eleven architects, appointed to examine the building, agreed that there was no danger from a similar accident in the future. This report the Council wished to have published that the attendance at the Exhibition might not be affected. Their request was granted.

CLVII[1]

To the Right Reverend and Reverend the
DEAN and CHAPTER of St. Paul's Cathedral

[May, 1791.]

The President and Council of the Royal
Academy having been informed that the Dean and
Chapter of St. Pauls have an intention of per-
mitting Monuments to be erected in that Cathedral,
take the liberty of offering their services in regu-
lating the disposition of those Monuments, examining the Sculptors Models determining the
magnitude of the figures and giving their advice
and assistance if required, on whatever affects the
beauty and decoration of the building.

For this purpose they propose to select from their
body a Committee, consisting of The President two
Historical Painters, two Sculptors, and two Architects;[2] who with the assistance of the Surveyor of
St. Pauls, will prepare the business necessary to be
laid before the Dean and Chapter, for their final
determination.

J REYNOLDS PRES[t]:

1 From the hitherto unpublished copy in the minutes of the
General Assembly for a meeting held May 5, 1791. The Dean
of St Paul's was Sir George (Pretyman) Tomline (1750–1827),
Bishop of Lincoln, and later Bishop of Winchester.
2 West and Hamilton, Nollekens and Banks, Dance and
Chambers, were elected to this committee. Their term was to
expire at the end of three years.

221

CLVIII[1]

To DR. SAMUEL PARR

Dear Sir,   London, May 31st, 1791.

I felt myself much flattered in receiving a letter[2] from Dr. Parr, and still more by its being a long one, and more still by the confidence which you have been pleased to repose in me: I may add, likewise, that a man is most successfully flattered by being supposed to possess virtues to which he has the least pretensions.

My critical skill, alas! I am afraid is entirely confined to my own profession. It would be in me the highest degree of impertinence to speak of your superior qualifications for this business as from my own judgment: it is my learned friends who have universally pointed you out as the only man qualified in all points for this task. That it is an arduous task I am well aware, and that you are alarmed at the difficulty is a presumption in favour of what may be expected from your head.

1 From *The Works of Samuel Parr*..., iv, London, 1828, 681 *et seq.* The recipient (1747–1825), famous pedagogue, had been requested by Seward to write the epitaph for Johnson's monument.

2 *Op. cit.* iv, 678 *et seq.*, in which Parr alludes to the difficulty of writing an epitaph which would be pleasing to all, asks Sir Joshua's opinion, and requests him to send him the dates of Johnson's birth and death and a list of subscribers to the monument.

A blind horse starts at no precipice. I have heard you speak of Dr. Johnson, and am therefore confident that you have nothing to seek in regard to sentiment; and in regard to your ability of expressing those sentiments in Latin, nobody has any doubt. You have, therefore, nothing to do but *"skrew your courage to the sticking place, and we'll not fail"*. Since I have stumbled by accident on this passage in Macbeth, I cannot quit it without observing that this metaphor is taken from a wheel engine, which, when wound up, receives a check that prevents it from running back.[1] The only check that I can imagine to prevent you from retreating from what I wish to consider as a private half-promise, would be its being publicly known that you had undertaken it. And then, as Dr. Johnson used to say, "what must be done, will be done".

I do not at all wonder at your being terrified at the difficulty: I am inclined to think that it is the most difficult of all compositions. Perhaps it is impossible to write an epitaph that shall be universally approved; or that shall not be open to some objection on one side or the other: even men of the best and most refined taste, are often unreasonable in their demands, and require (as I have seen connoisseurs do) an union of excellencies incompatible with each other.

The simplicity which you intend to adopt, and

[1] This note is not included in the "Variorum" *Macbeth*.

which is perfectly congenial to my own taste, will be criticised that it is not the lapidary style, that it wants dignity and stateliness, and so *vice versâ*.

Though I have great abhorrence of pertness or quaintness, either in the style or sentiment, yet perhaps an epitaph will admit of something of the epigrammatic turn. I remember once having made this observation to Edmund Burke, that it would be no bad definition of one sort of epitaphs, to call them grave epigrams. He repeated the words "*grave* epigrams", and gave me the credit of a pun, which I never intended.

I have no doubt but that you are surprised to receive a letter in this form. The truth is, this was intended only as a rough draft, but the weakness of my eyes must prove my excuse in not writing it over fair.

I shall enclose, if it will not make too large a packet for the post, the list of subscribers.

I am, with the greatest respect,

Your most humble and most
obedient servant,

JOSHUA REYNOLDS.

Dr. Johnson,
born Sept. 18, 1709,
died Dec. 13, 1784.

CLIX[1]

To DR. SAMUEL PARR

Dear Sir, London, July 11, 1791.

You may depend on having all your injunctions, relative to the inscription, punctually obeyed. We have great time before us. The statue is hardly yet begun, so that the inscription will not be wanted for at least these twelve months: in the meantime, you will probably have an opportunity of seeing the monument itself, and the place which it is to occupy in St. Paul's.

There would be, I think, a propriety in having on the scroll a Greek sentence, as it would imply at first sight that it is the monument of a scholar. Dr. Johnson was Professor of Ancient Literature to the Royal Academy. I could wish that this title might be on the monument: it was on this pretext that I persuaded the Academicians to subscribe a hundred guineas.[2] But I do not want to encroach on your department: you must ultimately determine its propriety.

1 From *The Works of Samuel Parr*..., iv, London, 1828, 686. It is in answer to a letter from Parr dated July 2 and is answered July 17. These two letters of Parr were first published by Leslie and Taylor (ii, 617 *et seq.*). The former is now in the Yale University Library, the latter in the possession of Gabriel Wells, Esq., of New York.

2 Sir Joshua's MS. account of his struggle with the Academy on this score, now in the possession of Gabriel Wells, Esq., was first published by Leslie and Taylor (ii, 610 *et seq.*).

I do not think that in any of my letters I have mentioned Mr. Windham's name,[1] which looks as if we did not see each other as often as we used to do, but this is not the case; I have shewn him all your letters, but as he expressed only general approbation, and the propriety of the whole being left to your judgment, I neglected telling you as much, which still I ought to have done.

I sent to Bacon the sculptor, to desire he would send me a sketch of the monument, which, if it comes in time, I will enclose it in this letter; if not, I will take the first opportunity of sending it to you.

I confess I am rather impatient to see the inscription; but still, not so much so as to wish in the least to break in upon any determination of yours. I must wait, likewise, for your orders respecting Mr. Seward;[2] as he has been active in this business, one would wish not to mortify him by neglect.

I am, with the greatest respect, yours sincerely,

J. REYNOLDS.

1 William Windham (1750–1810), the statesman, who was a member of the committee in charge of the monument. With him alone Parr wished Sir Joshua to consult on this business.
2 William Seward (1747–1799), man of letters. In his answer Parr allows Sir Joshua to take Seward also into his confidence. For a detailed account of Parr's negotiations with the committee *v.* Boswell's *Life*, iv, 444 *et seq.* and Wheatley's *Johnson's Monument and Parr's Epitaph on Johnson* (Johnson Club Papers, Second Series, London, 1920, 221 *et seq.*).

CLX[1]

To OZIAS HUMPHRY

September 24th, [1791.]

Sir Joshua Reynolds presents his compliments to Mr. Humphry and desires the honour of his company to dinner tomorrow.

CLXI[2]

To BENJAMIN WEST

Dear Sir   [November 10, 1791.]

I must request the favour of you to supply my place at the General Meeting held this Evening, I beg at the same time that You will acquaint the Academicians that however desirous I am & ever shall be to contribute every service in my power towards the prosperity of the Academy, yet as I feel myself incapable of serving the Office of President for the ensuing year, I think it necessary that this should be declared at the present Meeting,

1 From catalogue no. 457, issued in 1924 by the Messrs Maggs. The letter was written after 1769, when Reynolds was knighted. Since at this season in most of the previous years either Sir Joshua or the recipient was away from London, and since in the closing years of Sir Joshua's life Humphry was his constant companion (Northcote, ii, 248), I am led to infer that the note was written in 1791.
2 From the minutes of the General Assembly for a meeting held November 10, 1791. First published in Farington's *Memoirs of ...Sir Joshua Reynolds*, London, 1819, 116.

that the Academicians may have time to consider
between this & the tenth of December of a proper
successor.

                I am with great respect

                    Your most Obedᵗ: Servᵗ:

                       JOSHUA REYNOLDS. [1]

[1] Among the Reynolds papers in the Royal Academy is a hitherto
unpublished MS., which apparently was the first draft of this
letter. I print it with his own cancellations to show how he
composed a formal letter:

    "Tho my Eyes are much better than they have lately been
yet I am afraid to put them to the severe tryal of the business
of this Evening As such interruptions ~~to a man~~ are likely ~~often
to happen~~ to be more & more frequent I must beg leave to
recommend to the Academicians at the next General Election
That they would elect a President ~~that is likely~~ less liable to such
accidents

    "~~There~~ it is undoubtedly open to ridicule the declining an
honour ~~that is not nor can it be~~ before it is offerd, ~~nor am~~ but
~~it must be considered~~ as I have had had the honour annually
conferrd on me for these two and twenty years, it will not be
considerd as too presumptious to suppose that the same favour
would be continued ~~on the tenth of Dec next was I to wait for
that Election before I gave in~~ [*supra*, ~~in order then to give in~~]
~~my resignation it would be creating additional trouble to the
Academy,~~ another year but I thought it ~~therefore~~ more elegible
to run the risque of incurring the censure of this presumption
rather than give ~~this an~~ the additional trouble ~~of another
Election~~ to the Academicia[n]s of another Election I need not
repeat the regret which I feel in parting with the Academy."

    Though Sir Joshua was re-elected on December 10, he had
attended his last meeting; a few months later the secretary
entered the following note in his records: "On the 23ᴰ of Febʸ
'twixt Eight & Nine in the Evening, Died. Our worthy
President".

APPENDICES

APPENDIX I

Scattered throughout Sir Joshua's pocket-books are memoranda such as: "To write to Mr. Knight", "Writing to Mr. Hamiton", "Write to Mr. Gill", etc. Though some of these letters may never have been written, I have catalogued such remarks in order to furnish possible clues in determining the date or recipient of letters which may come to light in the future. The dates are of course approximate, and the names are given as Reynolds spelt them. I have also included letters which are mentioned in contemporary writings and those, sold at auctions, which I have been unable to locate. Where no reference is given, the note is from the pocket-books.

1750.	Miss Weston. (Two letters. *V. ante*, Letter VI.)
1750–1751.	Mrs. Palmer. (Leslie and Taylor, i, 39.)
	Mrs. Johnson. (*Ibid.*)
1755, Jan. 27–31.	Mr. Wilton.
June 23–28.	Lord Carisfort.
1757, Apr. 27.	Mr. Buller.
1759, Nov. 25.	Mr. Gill.
1761, June 3–4.	—(About Mrs. Pigot's Picture.)
1764, Oct. 5.	Mrs. Hood. (About Capt. Hood's Picture.)
1765, May 18.	Mr. Keppell.
1766, May 7.	Mr. Raton (?).
Nov. 18.	Mr. Ackland.

1767, Jan. 26.	Mr. Brett.
(spring?)	David Garrick(?). (Prior's *Life of Goldsmith*, ii, London, 1837, 151.)
July 13.	Thomas Percy. (A.L. 3rd person, sold at Sotheby's, April 10, 1895.)
Dec. 30.	Lord Maynard.
	Mrs. O'Brien.
	Mr. Clive.
	Capt. Collier.
	Mr. Gill.
	Mr. Gainsboro.
1768, Mar. 25.	Sister Palmer.
	Mr. Way.
	Lord Besborough.
June 20–21.	Mr. Fallowfill(?).
Oct. 24.	M. Doyen.
	Lord Arundell.
Nov. 21–27.	Rev. Mr. Morrison, Great Torrington.
	Miss Palmer, Great Torrington.
	Mr. Young, Great Torrington.
	Mr. Hoare, Bath.
	Mr. Gainsborough, Bath. (*Cf.* Leslie and Taylor, i, 312 n.)
Dec. 31.	Dr. Franklin.
	Mr. Hamiton.
1769, May 15–17.	Mr. Lutterell, Dunster Castle, Somersetshire. (About Miss Lutterell's picture.)
June 24.	Capt. Pownall (?).
	The Schoolmaster.
Dec. 5.	—(about the Statue.)

1770, Sep. 24–30.   Richard Johnson.
                     Dr. Young.
                     Barron Britain.
                     Mr. Don Wolmer (?).
                     Mr. Farr.
                     Mr. Bastard.
                     Mr. Veal.
                     Capt. Vincent.
                     Mr. Foot.
                     Mr. Manly.
            —   James Brunton. (Encouraging him
                     to study painting. *V.* Gwynn's
                     Northcote, 51.)

1771, Mar. 14.   Mr. Valtravers. (Council Minutes
                     under date.)
      Aug. 26.   Mr. Finch.
                     Mr. Shafto.
      Nov. 6–7.   Mr. Neugent.
      Dec. 18.   Duke of Dorset. (Council Minutes
                     under date.)
                     Sir William Hamilton. (*Id.*)

1772, Feb. 13–14.   Mr. Gill.
                     Madam Blanchard.
                     Capt. Orme.
      Feb. 29.   —(about Pictures sold at Auction.)
      Mar. 11–12.   Sir Robert Wilmot.
      Nov. 2.   Lord Sidney.
                     Mr. Child.

1773, Mar. 20.   Chamber[s].
      Mar. 26.   Mr. Rennich (?).
      Sep. 5.   Mr. Powels (?).
            —   Lord Ossory.

233

1773.	Duke of Dorset. Lord Palmerston. Lord Carlile.
—	Sir William Elford, Plympton. (About portrait. *V.* Leslie and Taylor, ii, 36.)
1775, Oct.	Lord Carlisle. (About pictures. *V. George Selwyn and his Contemporaries*, ed. Jesse, iii, London, 1882, 110.)
1777, Aug. 9.	Mr. Harding. Mr. Roth.
1778, Apr. 24.	—(A.L.S., 1 p. 4°, on 2nd leaf a Bill for two paintings, sold at Sotheby's, July 16, 1898, to the Messrs Maggs.)
Nov. 4.	Robert Lowth. (A.L. 3rd person, thanking him for his present of *Isaiah. V.* Catalogue 454, item 2113, issued in 1924 by the Messrs Maggs. *Cf. ante*, Letter XLVI.)
1779 (?).	Lord Townshend. (Requesting living for Joseph Palmer. *V.* Northcote, ii, 41.)
1780, Sep. 29.	Mr. French. (A.L.S., 1 p. 4°, thanking him for a gift of partridges; sold at Sotheby's, July 24, 1929, to John Heise, Esq.)
Nov. 22 (?).	Jonathan Shipley. (Congratulating him on his election to the Club. *V.* Lord Teignmouth's *Memoirs of Sir William Jones*, London, 1804, 194.)

1781. Warren Hastings. (Recommending William Johnson. *V. ante*, Letter LIV.)

1782, March. William Mason. (Stating he has finished annotating Fresnoy. *V.* Leslie and Taylor, ii, 352 n.)

June 18. Lord Tenet.

— Thomas Gainsborough. ("Sending a hundred guineas" for the *Girl with Pigs* "with half as many elegant compliments on the work of the artist". *V.* Whitley's *Life of Gainsborough*, London, 1915, 186. *Cf. ante*, Letter CI.)

1783. Lord Macartney. (Introducing Mr Smith. *V. ante*, Letter LXXIII.)

1784, May 18–20. Lord Spencer/Bristil/Bucks.

June 15–16. a Lord (?).

Aug.–Sep. James Boswell. (About Boswell's "pious negociation" in regard to Johnson. *V.* Boswell's *Life*, iv, 348.)

Samuel Johnson. (*Id.*)

Samuel Johnson. (*Id.* 368.)

1785, Apr. Thomas Warton. (About poet-laureateship. *V.* Leslie and Taylor, ii, 472.)

June 25. Thomas Percy. (Promises to help Goldsmith's brother. *V.* Balderston's *History...of Percy's Memoir*, Cambridge, 1926, 26.)

Sep. 10. Mr. De Gree. (*V. ante*, Letter XC.)

— Mr. Cunningham. (*V. ante*, Letter XCIV.)

1785, Sep. 26.   Mr. De Gree. (*V. ante*, Letter xcii.)

1787, Jan.   Lord Cornwallis. (Recommending William Johnson. *V.* unpublished letters of Mary Palmer.)

June 26.   Mr. Serres.

Dec. 2.   Marquis of Buckingham. (A.L.S., 1 p. 4°, sold at Sotheby's January 15, 1898, and again April 15, 1899.)

Dec. 7.   Joseph Palmer. (A.L.S., 3 pp. 4°, condoling with him on the loss of his patron, the Duke of Rutland. Sold at the Anderson Galleries, N.Y., December 1, 1920.)

1788, Feb. 11.   Lord Salisbury. (A.L.S., 1 p. 4°, soliciting a ticket for the trial of Hastings. Sold at the Anderson Galleries, N.Y., April 30, 1906.)

June 16.   The Hon. Shute Barrington. (A.L. 3rd person, 1/2 p. 4°, in the possession of R. B. Adam, Esq., of Buffalo.)

Nov. 24–27.   Lord Lifford, Loxley Hall near Uttoxeter, Staffordshire. (About Picture and Print.)

Dec. 25.   John Bacon. (A.L.S., 1 p. 8°, asking him to visit Westminster Abbey to inspect the vacant niche provided for a whole-length statue of Dr Johnson in the manner of Pythagoras, with a request for an estimate of the cost. Sold at Sotheby's, June 21, 1922.)

1789, Jan. 14.   Mr. Pott.

1789, Apr. 1.   Benjamin West. (Asking him to present Letters CXXVII and CXXVIII to their Majesties. *V.* Council Minutes under date.)

June 2.   Mr. Knight.

Dec. (?).   —(Circular letters about Johnson's monument. *V. Letters of James Boswell,* Oxford, 1924, 386.)

1790, Feb. 6.   Mr. Nicoll. (Item 583 in catalogue 242, issued in 1908 by the Messrs Maggs.)

Feb. 7 (?).   Sir William Chambers. (About the choice of a Professor of Perspective. *V.* folio 10 in unpublished MSS. of Sir Joshua's *Apologia* in the Royal Academy.)

Feb. 11.   John Richards. (*V. ante,* p. 199, n. 1.)

March.   Lord Warwick. (*V. post,* Appendix III, Letter K.)

Apr. 20.   Mr. Browne. (A disappointed artist. *V.* Council Minutes under date.)

—   Count Woronzow. (Concerning the gift of Catherine II. *V.* unpublished letter of Mary Palmer, dated Aug. 17, 1790.)

—   Thomas Lawrence. (Asking for address of Roth, a journeyman painter of drapery. *V. Sir Thomas Lawrence's Letter-Bag,* London, 1906, 16.)

1791, Jan. 18.   James Boswell. (Inviting him to dinner. *V. Letters of James Boswell,* Oxford, 1924, 415.)

1791, July.

Dr. Thomas Barnard. (Asking him to become chaplain to the Royal Academy. *V.* Leslie and Taylor, ii, 622.)

Oct. 14.

Sir William Chambers. (Asking him to act as chairman for a Council Meeting. *V.* Leslie and Taylor, ii, 621.)

n.d.

Dr. William Hunter. (A.L. 3rd person, 1 p. 4°, sold at Sotheby's June, 1874, lot 3686.)
Hannah More. (A.L. 3rd person, 1 p. 4°, thanking her for an admission order to the theatre. Sold at Sotheby's July 13, 1896, and at the Anderson Galleries, N.Y., March 22, 1915.)
John Nichols. (A.L.S., 1 p. 4°, sold by Stan V. Henkels, of Philadelphia, June 2, 1916.)

APPENDIX II

LETTERS ATTRIBUTED TO SIR JOSHUA

The Henry E. Huntington Library and Art Gallery possesses an unpublished, undated note, which commences: "Sir Joshua and Mrs. Reynolds present their compliments to Dr. and Mrs. Percy". A comparison of the handwriting with that in letters of Sir Joshua's sister Frances, who served for a number of years as his house-keeper, proves beyond a doubt that it was she who wrote the note.

Two unpublished letters to James Northcote, now in the possession of Henry Fatio, Esq., of Geneva, have been considered as Sir Joshua's, but the fact that they were actually written by the artist Prince Hoare has been ably proved by William T. Whitley, Esq., in an article in *The Times Literary Supplement* for February 12, 1920 (xix, 106).

Northcote (ii, 148 *et seq.*) believes that an anonymous letter written in May, 1783, to James Barry, was the joint production of Burke and Reynolds. The theory, however, remains unproved.

An unpublished, undated letter to John Liston, the actor (*d.* 1846), was attributed to Sir Joshua in Sotheby's catalogue for a sale held November 17, 1908. Since the letter refers to Liston's acting, and since he did no acting in Sir Joshua's lifetime, I infer that the writer was the dramatist Frederic Reynolds, who was closely associated with Liston's career.

APPENDIX III

A[1]

From

MRS. ELIZABETH HOOPER HUMPHRY

S[r]   Honiton aprill 24 1765

as I never Rec[d] one Letter from my son since he
has been In London but he Inform me In it of the
many favors he is continually receveing from you and
as a mothers regard makes her esteem favors conferd
on a child more then if done to her self I take the
Liberty to return you my sincerest thanks and as the
Inclosd is of our own manufacturing as a small Instance of gratitude your acceptance of it will confer an
additionall obligation on

S[r]

your most oblidg Humble servant

ELIZ HUMPHRY

B

From MRS. CHARLOTTE LENNOX

May 20, 1773.

(Requesting an interview. In the possession of
R. B. Adam, Esq., of Buffalo. In his pocket-book Sir
Joshua notes an appointment with her for seven
o'clock on May 24. The letter is to be published in
Miss Miriam R. Small's study of the author of *The
Female Quixote*.)

1 From the original in the possession of the Royal Academy.
(*Correspondence of Ozias Humphry*, i, f. 88.) *Cf. ante*, Letter VIII.

C[1]

From WILLIAM GARDINER

Sir   *Richmond May the 2ᵈ., 1774—

Having been so fortunate as to make Two Astro-
nomical Discoveries, which will probably incline
Posterity to wish for a lively Resemblance of me, I
would willingly avail myself of your masterly Pencil
to gratify them therein.

If you should incline to become my *Magnus Apollo*
in this Attempt, I will communicate to you the Ways
and Means I would recommend to make the Portrait
acceptable, by the Introduction of Machinery, of which
I can furnish you with great Choice.

My feeble State of Health will not permit me to sit
to you in London, so if you should accede to my Pro-
posal, I hope it will prove agreable to you to take the
Face here, upon your next Retreat to our little *Alps.*—
I shall be attending to know your Pleasure in due
Season, and am with Regard

Sir

Yʳ. most obedᵗ. Servᵗ—

Wᴹ. GARDINER

---

1 From the original in the possession of Rupert Colomb, Esq.,
now lent to the Royal Academy. The portrait was never
painted.

D[1]

From GIUSEPPE PELLI

Sir   *Florence. Nov. 21 1775

Sig[r]. Luigi Siries has presented to his Royal High-
ness The Portrait of yourself painted for the celebrated
collection of this Royal Gallery. Tho we were not un-
aquainted with the reputation which you bear in your
Profession yet this Portrait reduces to evident demon-
stration what we before knew only by fame. My
Intention Sir Joshua is not to praise you. your merit
is too much known to stand in need of it. I am orderd
only by the express commands of my Royal Master to
assure you of the particular satisfaction with which he
has receiv'd this work of your hand and the pleasure
with which he order'd me to arrange it among the
Portraits of the most illustrious Painters, which I have
according done by placing it in the *first* Room In this
situation, tho confronted with the[2] with the Productions
of the Artists of all Nations, you suffer nothing by the
comparison on the contrary acquire fresh glory. The
Dilettanti and Professors who run with eagerness to
admire it find in it, all the beauties of Rembrands
manner carried to perfection, and I am very happy to
find that the first Portrait of an English Painter in this
most inestimable collection of my Sovereign, is yours;
and the Portrait too of him who so justly presides over
the Royal Academy of London.

1 From Sir Joshua's translation in the possession of Rupert
  Colomb, Esq., now lent to the Royal Academy. The letter is
  endorsed: "A translation of the Letter of Sign[r] Giuseppe Pelli
  Director of the Royal Gallery at Florence to Sir Joshua
  Reynolds". *Cf. ante*, Letter XXXIV. The Italian original is also
  in Mr Colomb's possession.
2 The first page of the MS. ends at this point.

At the same time that it shews what progress Painting has made, it likewise shews how much tast and intelligence those acquire who come to study, or as you have done, finish their studies in Italy, which is confirmed by the Drawings of our Divine Micheagnolo which you have not distaind to hold in your hand.

Sir Joshua I hope you will value this testimony of the esteem which the Arch Duke Grand Duke has for you, and I think myself much honourd with the employment allotted me of explaining to you the sentiments, of an Enlightend and amiable Prince, & who knows how to set a proper value upon a person of your merit.

I take this opportunity of declaring myself one of the admirers of your extraordinary talent and to offer you my services; Employ me therefore in the execution of your commands and give me leave to subscribe myself with the greatest respect

> Sir
>> Your most devoted and obliged servant
>>> GIUSEPPE PELLI
>>> Director of the Royal Gallery.

To Sir Joshua Reynolds
London

E[1]

From WILLIAM MASON

Dear S[r]   Aston Aug[st] 25th, 1776

I am much obligd to you for being so merciful to my second Book, when both the subject & the blank

[1] From the original in the possession of Rupert Colomb, Esq., now lent to the Royal Academy.

verse it was written in were neither of them favorites of yours. The objection you make about the address to Coloring, I know will be made by evry body but *House Painters & Gardiners*; and as you are neither the one nor the other (God be thankd) I think it was very proper in you to make it, But Brown who knows how necessary the *house* Painter is to the completion of his Art, approves this Passage extremely, and indeed this matter is very essential to the subject. Was I to be calld in to improve the Ground before your Villa at Richmond. I should want the assistance of all the House Painters in Town to hide the Alms houses & stables that stood in my way, and, unless they could make them the exact hue of the neibouring Herbage, My Art would be nonplust. You see from this familiar instance how necessary the Invocation in question was to the subject there treated. But enough of nonsense. Mr Doughty who was stopt here two days for want of a conveyance. employd himself last Saturday in drawing a portrait of my friend Mr Whitehead, who happend to be with me. He producd so good a likeness with so much facility that he has pleasd me highly and from this instance of his great improvement since he has had the good fortune to be your Pupil, I am very sanguine in my hopes that your kindness towards him will not be thrown away. He seems to have a very just sense of that kindness, and so long as he retains that, he will be assurd of all the encouragement that I can either give him or procure him. Believe me to be

Dear S^r

most cordially yours

W MASON

My best Compl^mts to Miss Reynolds.

F[1]

From VALENTINE GREEN

*May 31st 1783.

Sir!   Newman Street.

The steps I had taken to obtain the use of the Portrait of Mrs. Siddons, I looked upon so orderly, and the Answers I received so conclusive in favour of my Application from Yourself, Mrs. Siddons and Mr. Sheridan, of which You are already fully informed, that I could not but be surprised at Your telling me in the presence of M[r]. Whitford on Wednesday last that "*I could not have the picture, Mrs. Siddons having Written to You, recommending another Artist, to have it done in another manner*". The inconsistency, improbability, and injustice of such a determination required that I should investigate the matter more closely, and endeavour to trace whence such an obstruction to my claim had arisen. I accordingly went that same Afternoon to Mr. Haward, (the Artist said to be recommended by M[rs]. Siddons) and received a very candid Account of what he knew; and from him I learnt that his Application to You for the picture was gladly received and consented to by you; and that he neither saw nor heard from Mrs. Siddons on the Subject.—In this decision it appears, therefore, that no hesitation on Your part was made whether "the choice of the Engraver lay with You" or not, and that it was finished at once without Regard or Reference to any other opinion; and in preference to a prior claim, notwithstanding the *utmost caution* was necessary to be used when I

1 From the original in the possession of Rupert Colomb, Esq., now lent to the Royal Academy. *Cf. ante*, Letter LXX.

245

applied, and notwithstanding Your Written promise to me, "if *the choice of the Engraver depended on you, that my first Application was certainly to be remembered*". But this promise, it seems, was described by you to Mr. Haward as amounting to "*nothing conclusive*" although You knew the acquiescence of Mrs. Siddons and of Mr. Sheridan was solicited by me, and founded by them on that promise.

With still less reason to be satisfied with the information I had received I determined on farther inquiries into the business, and accordingly, Yesterday Morning, waited on Mrs. Siddons. The information I there received from Mr. Siddons, and from his Report of her Answers, was uniform with the explicit manner in which she first expressed her concurrence in my having the picture, that she had never concerned herself about the manner in which it was to be executed, nor farther interested herself about the Artist who was to engrave it than what she had already done in concurring with my former Application to her, conceiving Your choice of the Engraver had been determined in the answer you gave me.— Hence it appears, that Mrs. Siddons never did Write, or even Speak to You in favour of another Artist to engrave the picture in any manner, and that my Interest in the matter was never meant to be opposed at all by Her.

I next possessed Mr. Sheridan with the state of the case, and found his opinion equally unbiassed. He had never interested himself at all about the manner in which it was to be done; on the contrary, he had called on You to speak of my Application to him, in conformity to what his Note had assured me he meant to do, (which Note I inclosed to You,) but Your being then engaged he did not see You. In conclusion, he told Me he meant to see You, to inform himself fully on this Matter, and as far as he can to set it on its right footing.

In this instance it also appears You had been left wholly at liberty to make choice of an Artist, and from Your Answer to Me which I shewed to Mr. Sheridan it could appear to him in no other light than that I was to have the portrait if no objection should arise from him or Mrs. Siddons.

It was my intention from what hints You threw out in Your Reply to my Application, and which I had repeatedly mentioned to others, to have the plate executed in whatever manner Yourself, Mrs. Siddons, or Mr. Sheridan might determine on when the picture was finished, and to have commissioned any Artist that might have been mentioned to have done it. You are not to be informed that this practice is common; and that by that means the proprietorship of that plate would have been equally secured to Me as if I myself had done it.

If therefore in an instance like the present a Subject should arise which should promise a Reward to an Engraver to produce, He who had executed a great number of your works, and that too at a considerable loss in many of them; whose Claim was prior to every other, and whose claim was complied with on all hands, should surely have been secured in it. In this situation I stand; and I may now demand that as a *Right*, which I originally solicited as a *favour* from You. The manner in which that claim has been set aside will not bear examining; and I am hurt that such means were resorted to to effect it when a civil negative in the first instance would have answered the purpose so much better. It is now become necessary that the whole matter should be reconsidered by You, and that strict justice should be rendered on all hands.

The Attention You bestow on Mr. Haward reflects a lustre on Your discrimination of high Abilities; but that it should be exerted at the expence of others cannot, will not be allowed. And even a less qualified Artist than myself would revolt at the idea of taking the Refuse of Your Gallery under such circumstances.

At all events it may be worthy Your consideration in future to give unequivocal Answers to plain propositions, and so avoid the Risk of sporting with any Man's temper where his personal and professional Characters are concerned. I shall wait the Result of Your determination on this matter; and sincerely hope it may reflect as much honour on Your discernment as a Man, as the execution of the Subject in question will unquestionably add honour to You as an Artist. And let it be remembered that it is the first Character I am now seeking after, and I have dropped all consideration of the last.

I am Sir,

Your humble Servant

V. GREEN[1]

---

1 After this letter had been set up, I discovered that it had been published in *The Literary Gazette*, 1822, 85, together with Green's dignified answer to what is Letter LXX in this collection.

G¹

From THOMAS GAINSBOROUGH

[1782.]

...I think myself highly honor'd and much obliged to you for this singular mark of your favour; I may truly say that I have brought my Piggs to a fine market....

H²

From RICHARD GRAVES

Sir,   Claverton near Bath 26 Dec 1785

I have taken, I fear, an unwarrentable [liberty] in a[ddress]ing a gentleman, as much distinguish'd by his litterary abilit[ies as] by his consummate knowledge of the Fine Arts. But your k[nown] attachment to the subject of the inclosed, will, I hope, operate in my favour. Indeed, I should not have given *you*, Sir, this trouble, if I had known Mr. Boswel's address: who, I find, is preparing a voluminous History of Dr. Johnson's Life. And if (as is usual in works of that kind) there should be any Appendix or Collection of panegyrical or threnodial verses, in which a thing of this sort could be introduced, I should be greatly flattered if it should be thought worthy of such distinction— Though it was written at the time of Dr. Jˢ death, as I have never shewn it to any one, I cannot judge of its merit. If it has any, it is the comprising, in

---

1 From Sotheby's catalogue for a sale held December 2, 1910 (lot 26). *Cf. ante*, Appendix I, under 1782.

2 From the original in the possession of Gabriel Wells, Esq., of New York, who also owns the elegy. Boswell did not make use of it.

tolerably smooth rhymes, the chief particulars of that great man's excellence.

Though I never saw, I was not entirely unknown to, Dr. Johnson & by means of a common friend, had an obliging message from him about 2 years since, but he was gone into ye country before I got to Town to ye royal exhibition— I was of Pembroke College, before I was elected to All Soul's, where I early began to admire him, for his excelent translation of Pope's Messiah.

As no one likes anonymous Letters, I make no scruple of trusting my Name, without fear of ridicule, to a gentleman of your candid & liberal character. I am a person of no consequence, but have been a little known, by my long intimacy with ye late Mr. Shenstone, & am, Sir, with great esteem,

y^r most obed ser

RIC^D GRAVES

P. S. As I am a volunteer in this address, I have no right to, nor require any answer.

J^1

From the Right Reverend THOMAS PERCY

Dear Sir,   Dromore, March 20. 1786

I blush to think how long I have let your very obliging Letter remain unanswerd, but I delay'd writing till I could find a Mem^dum. I had made relating to the amount between D^r. Johnson & me w^ch.

---

1 From a copy of the original in the possession of the Johnson Society, Lichfield. The memorandum shows that on November 10, 1778, Johnson lent Percy £150 at 5 per cent. For Percy's interest in Maurice Goldsmith *v.* Miss Balderston's *History . . . of Percy's Memoir*, Cambridge, 1926.

after my several removals from Lond^n. to Carlisle, & from Carlisle to Ireland did not turn up, till lately. I send it on the other side, together with a Draught for the Interest due to the end of the last half year to Francis Barber. When you wrote last you expressed your kind Intentions of recommending a Subscription for D^r. Goldsmith's Brother to the Club. May I beg to know the Result? I shall willingly subscribe to D^r. Johnson's Monum^t & desire you will deduct my subscription from whatever money you may receive for Maurice Goldsmith, whose Proposals I sent to M^r. Malone. As I have not seen any other Members of the Club since I left Dublin last midsummer & as I shall pass the Spring months here I have not been able to promote the Monum^t. Subscription, as otherwise I sh^d. have gladly have done, to show my readiness to obey any commands of yours being ever Dear Sir

Your faithful obliged servant

THO: DROMORE

P S I just got a glimpse of M^r. Palmer last summer in Dublin, but he suddenly left town before I could press him to favour me with his Company here, as in Dublin I only had Lodgings

K[1]

From LORD WARWICK

Dear Sr *Warwick Castle March 25th. 1790.

I received the favor of your Letter this morning but too late to answer it by the return of the Post. I inclose a draft for the Achilles. In regard to the

[1] From the original in the possession of Rupert Colomb, Esq., now lent to the Royal Academy.

other Picture I am far from thinking myself a proper Judge of its Value. all I feel is that tho' I accknowledge its Merit as a picture I have my objections to its Subject—& therefore have no wish to possess it at more than the price you mention— But if it will be the least use to you in any Exchange with Mr. Desenfans I beg you will not think yourself in any degree engaged to give me the offer of it. And I assure you I shall equaly think myself obliged to you for wishing to let me have it. I beg you will not give yourself the trouble of answering this for if I do not hear from you I will send the money to you next week—

I congratulate you on the proper and honerable manner in wʰ you are placed where no one has so good a title to preside & I am Dear Sʳ with great Regard   Your faithful & Obedᵗ Servant

                                                        WARWICK

P. S. Having just paid £20,000 for an Estate I believe I am not in Cash at Messʳˢ Drummonds but as I expect my Steward here today I will send the money to you by Mondays post should this be the case.

Lᴵ

From GENERAL JOHN BURGOYNE

Sir   Hertford Street May 1ˢᵗ, 1790

After what had passed relative to Mr Maquignon I should hardly have beleived, upon less evidence than my eye sight, that his picture was not in the Exhibition. From the modesty of his pretensions & the humility of his station, he must submit in silence: I am

---

1 From the original in the possession of Rupert Colomb, Esq., now lent to the Royal Academy. *Cf.* Leslie and Taylor, ii, 587.

too much implicated in the circumstances of his ill-treatment, & feel my share too forcibly, to follow that example. Indeed, Sir, these circumstances are so very extraordinary, that I doubt my own recollection as well as the representation of other persons; & I therefore must trouble you with a recapitulation of the most material, & would know from you whether it is correct as far as you are concerned.

Mr. Maquignon while his picture was in hand was encouraged by the favourable opinion of many distinguished judges, among which yours made him most proud: Your praise was of the first value, & as it was accompanied with notice of his faults he thought it sincere. His picture was rejected at the Academy. The Academiciens were unquestionably the proper arbiters in the competition of the candidate artists, and however disappointed in his hopes, he had no right to complain. Neither did he; nor did I in his name, when I waited on you upon the subject. I only lamented that he was deprived of an honour that I knew would have operated upon his disposition as an excitement to study & labour, much more powerfully than any restraint upon his ambition would do, however kindly intended to him, or judicious when applied to young men of more self conceit. I stated to you also, how decidedly however improperly, the rejection of his picture would be regarded by his family as a proof of his incapacity, & how materially he might be injured in the income hitherto allotted for his years of study.

Upon these & other considerations, among which were some comparative merits of the composition, you obligingly engaged to me your good offices for its being accepted upon a reconsideration of the Committee.

Some days after, when I understood there had been another meeting I wrote to you to know the issue. The

253

answer I received by my servant, was, an apology for not writing, & a message in positive terms that "what I had wished was done, & the picture was received". In confirmation of this, when Mr. Maquignon waited on you the next day to express his gratitude, you assured him, as he reported to me, not only that "his picture was received", but that "to make amends for his former disappointment, you had taken care it should be hung in a good light"; & you added, as he also reported, the most flattering expressions of encouragement & protection.

So much, Sir, for the facts I had to submit to you: now for their consequences. The first was, that from a natural, & not an unbecoming pride this cajoled young man immediately communicated his success to his family—with whom probably by this time he must stand in the light of a vein coxcomb who has imposed upon himself, or as something worse than coxcomb who has endeavoured to impose upon them for the purpose of extracting money from their credulity.

Another consequence to which he has been exposed by this disappointment of promise is of a more trivial nature, but one not unproductive of vexation to an ingenuous mind. You well know how the character of M^{rs}. Candour abounds in this town in breeches as well as petticoats. Several of this cast were of course very forward to lament the fatal insertion of the name of Maquignon in the *black book*, with all the concern of malice & the insult of pity To them with a pride again natural & excusable, he gave at the time a flat contradiction referring them to my word & to yours. What is now his case? With his family, his acquaintance, all the circle of his little world he must appear to have asserted what is not true, or to affix upon one or both of us that imputation.

As to the *black book* itself, exposed as I am informed to every inspector, I confess I was much surprised to hear of it. I had imagined that the rejected pictures dropt quietly into oblivion like unpassed bills in parliament; but if this account be just, I am to understand that the Academy have a catalogue of disgrace as open as that of desert.

I come last, Sir, to my own resentment. And I have all the revenge I seek, when I make this representation to that liberal & benevolent heart which I have ever conceived & am still anxious to beleive you to possess. I am sure you cannot but regret the having trifled with the feelings of an honest & industrious youth whose first desire of life was to merit your protection. His despondency, not upon his failure, but upon the cruel manner of treating it, has been very near carrying him to a renunciation of the pencil, as well as of respect of the Academy for ever. The only consolation I have endeavoured to administer to him is one I beleive to be justly founded—viz—That his ill success arises not from his own defects but from the want of a more important patron than myself; that patronage & partiality are the only means by which a student can obtain a place in the exhibition is evident to every man who compares some of the works received with some that have been refused; that in regard to his Germanicus in particular it would have made a good foil to the pictures of the great masters, but not quite so perfect an one, as at least twenty that might be pointed out for which it has helped to make room.

Dear Sir Joshua   May 6ᵗʰ, 1790

After having left this letter five days unfinished, I now confess I wrote it in great anger; but upon reflection I have too great value for your talents & your virtues not to be placable.

I have the honour to be
Dear Sir
Your most obedient & most Humble Servant
J. BURGOYNE

M^r
From SIR WILLIAM CHAMBERS

Dear Sir   *Royal Academy May 26' 1790

I am very much Surprised to find a picture taken out of the Exhibition by Your private Order, Contrary to a positive law of the Academy, it is a precedent which may be attended with very ill consequences, and a Stretch of power in You, which it will be difficult to Justify You had an excuse at hand, and I cannot help wondering You did not Make use of it.

I am very truly
D^r S^r
Your most Obedient h^e Servt
W^M CHAMBERS

1 From the original in the possession of Rupert Colomb, Esq., now lent to the Royal Academy. Sir Joshua has endorsed it: "Sir Wm Chamber/Duke of Glocester/Picture/May 27/1790".

N[1]

From HENRIETTA BATTIER

Sir   *Dublin, Sep[r] 8th: 1790—

I hope the grateful Sincerity of my design, will excuse to the Heart of Doctor Johnsons friend its other imperfections, And tho Silenceing your Judgement find an Advocate in your good nature, For that great Men make great Allowances, The Ever to be lamented Johnson taught me— I was Honourd with his Friendship, and tho a Stranger in London, His Name was a Bulwark to my Endeavours. I hoped to have made my Children lisp it.— Forgive me, Sir, were I to follow the Dictates of my Heart, in telling you of his goodness, I should forget the post and write a Volume

I beg a Line, in hopes of Hearing that you are not Displeas'd at the Receipt of this little Pacquet, and am, Sir, with my best wishes to the Soul of genius in your person—   Sir

Your Dutiful and

Obliged Servant

HENRIETTA BATTIER

If Honour'd with an ans[r] please to direct for me to Rev[d] Dean Paul Great Britain Street

1 From the original in the Yale University Library. "This little Pacquet" contains *An Epitaph on the late Doctor Samuel Johnson*, which she wished to be carved on his monument.

APPENDIX III

O[1]

From THOMAS RICKMAN

*No 4 Upper Marylebone Street

Sir   *July 19— 1791—

When Doctor Johnson died, I wrote the following Epitaph upon him, and now hearing his monument is about to be erected, I offer it, to the conductors of it—

I am Sir Y^r hu S^t

THOS CLIO RICKMAN

An answer would be esteem'd a favour!

P

From MRS. JORDAN

(Sold at Sotheby's, June 14, 1899. *V.* catalogue, 61.)

Q

From MRS. BURKE

(Sold at Sotheby's, November 10, 1899. *V.* catalogue, 50. *Cf. ante,* Letter XXXVII.)

R

From —

(Sending some Rhenish wine from Rotterdam. Sold at Sotheby's, November 10, 1899. *V.* catalogue, 50.)

1 From the original in the possession of Gabriel Wells, Esq., of New York. The writer (1761–1834), bookseller and friend to Thomas Paine, enclosed an epitaph of fourteen lines.

APPENDIX IV

RECIPIENTS OF SIR JOSHUA'S LETTERS

(Numbers refer to letters in this edition, dates to those which are listed in Appendix I.)

Ackland, Mr., 1766
Arundell, Lord, 1768
Astle, Thomas, LXXIV

Bacon, John, CXXXII, 1788
Banks, Sir Joseph, XLVII, CXLVIII
Barnard, Thomas, 1791
Barrington, Lord, LII
Barrington, Shute, 1788
Barry, James, XII
Bastard, Mr., 1770
Beattie, James, XXV, LXI
Besborough, Lord, 1768
Birch, George, CXXII
Blanchard, Madam, 1772
Bonomi, Giuseppe, CXVIII, CXXXIII
Boswell, James, XIV, LXXXVI, CIX, 1784, 1791
Boydell, John, CXI
Brett, Mr., 1767
Britain, Barron, 1770
Browne, John, 1790
Brunton, James, 1770
Buckingham, Marquis of, 1787
Buller, Mr., 1757
Bunbury, Sir Charles, XVII
Burke, Edmund, LVII, LVIII

Cadell, Thomas, CLIII, CLV
Calze, *v.* Cunningham
Carisfort, Lord, 1755
Carlisle, Lord, 1773, 1775

Catherine II, Empress, CXLIII
Chambers, Sir William, CXXVI, CXXXIV, CXXXV, 1773, 1790, 1791
Charlotte, Queen, CXXVIII
Child, Mr., 1772
Clive, Mr., 1767
Collier, Capt., 1767
Collingwood, Thomas, LX
Cornwallis, Lord, 1787
Cosway, Richard, CXXIX
Crabbe, George, LXVII
Cribb, William, CLII
Cunningham, Edmund Francis, XCIV, XCVI, 1785

Daulby, Daniel, XL
De Gree, M., 1785
Dorset, Duke of, 1771, 1773
Doyen, M., 1768

Edgcumbe, Lord, V
Elford, Sir William, 1773

Fallowfill, Mr., 1768
Farr, Mr., 1770
Farr, Dr. Samuel, XXXIII
Finch, Mr., 1771
Foot, Mr., 1770
Franklin, Dr., 1768
French, Mr., 1780
Fuller, Stephen, LXXV

Gainsborough, Thomas, 1767, 1768, 1782

259   17-2

INDEX

Ackland, Mr., 231
Adam, R. B., 40 n., 61 n., 75 n., 214 n., 236, 240
Aeneid, 49 n., 174 n.
Agar, Wellbore E., 164
Akerman, Mr., 128
Algiers, the Dey of, 4 n., 5
Anderdon, J. H., 155 n., 215 n.
Anderson Galleries, 41 n., 236, 238
Ariosto, 79 n.
Arundell, Lord, 232
Ash, John, 182
Ashburnham, John, Earl, 150
Astle, Thomas, 108
Astley, John, xi, 10, 12
Athenaeum, 48 n., 50 n.ʼ
Aufrere, George, 27

Bacon, Sir Francis, 117
Bacon, John, 110, 191, 226, 236
Balderston, K. C., xvii
Banks, Sir Joseph, 67, 99, 211, 212 n.
Banks, Thomas, 221 n.
Barber, Francis, 251
Barnard, John, 202 n.
Barnard, Thomas, 140, 238
Barrett, O. R., 59 n.
Barrington, Hon. Samuel, 74
Barrington, Hon. Shute, 74, 236
Barrington, William Wildman, Viscount, 74
Barry, James, 16, 37 n., 239
Bartolozzi, Francesco, 88, 148
Barwell, Richard, 76
Bastard, Mr., 233
Battier, Henrietta, 257
Beattie, James, 39, 90
Beresford, Hon. Mrs., 35 n.
Bernini, 161

Bertie, Emily, 171 n.
Bessborough, Lord, *v.* Ponsonby
Bingham, Charles, Baron Lucan, 131, 169 n.
Bingham, Lavinia, Lady Spencer, 169
Bingham, Margaret Smyth, Lady Lucan, 76, 111, 123, 131, 169 n.
Biondi, 163, 175
Birch, George, 182
Blakeney, William, 6
Blanchard, Madam, 233
Bleackley, Horace, 29 n.
Bodleian Library, 209 n.
Bonapaduli, Marquis of, 125 n., 159, 162, 165
Bonomi, Giuseppe, 178, 192 n., 193
Bonomi, J. I., 193 n.
Boothby, Sir William, 31
Boston Public Library, 108 n.
Boswell, James, xv; letters to, 127, 167, 235, 237; love of accuracy, xvii; dines with Painter-Stainers, 167; sees execution at Newgate, 127; owes Percy a letter, 201; member of committee for Johnson's monument, 212 n.; writes Malone, 214; his *Johnsoniana*, 140; his *Journal*, 140 n.; his *Life of Johnson*, xxii, 211, 249; cited, 32 n., 41 n., 57 n., 67 n., 101 n., 128 n., 164 n., 173 n., 179 n., 181 n., 205 n.
Boswell, Mrs. James, 179 n.
Boydell, John, 170, 174, 213, 214
Bradner, L., 95 n.

263

Gardiner, William, 241
Garrick, David, 40–42, 232
Genlis, Comtesse de, 126
Gentleman's Magazine, xi, 100 n.,
138 n., 151 n., 212 n.
George II, 13 n., 150 n.
George III, his interest in the
R.A., 22, 23, 26, 27, 176,
177, 180, 194, 197; his re-
storation to health, 186–188,
237; mentioned, xx, 9 n.,
46 n., 84, 112, 113, 170,
186
George IV, 124
Germain, Lady Betty, 27
Gibbon, Edward, xiv, 39 n.,
97 n., 181
Gill, Mr., 231–233
Gilpin, William, 217
Goldsmith, Maurice, 235,
250 n., 251
Goldsmith, Oliver, xi, xiv, 15,
44 n., 61, 102 n., 181 n.,
235, 251
Goodspeed's Book Shop, 31 n.
Grafton, Duke of, 71 n.
Granby, *v.* Manners
Granger, James, 46
Graves, Richard, 249
Green, Valentine, 103, 245,
248 n.
Grenville, George, Marquis of
Buckingham, 124, 236
Grenville, George, 124 n.
Greville, Hon. Charles, 171
Griffin, William, 45
Guido, 18, 152
Gunning, Maria and Eliza-
beth, 11, 12
Gwatkin, R. G., 54 n., 78 n.,
105 n., 189 n.
Gwatkin, R. L., 78, 98, 105,
106, 189, 190, 202

Gwatkin, Mrs. R. L., *v.* Theophila Palmer
Gwatkin, Theophila, 105, 189,
190, 202
Gwyn, Col., 54 n.

Hambleton, Miss, 11
Hamilton, Charles, 122 n.
Hamilton, Gavin, 38, 164,
221 n.
Hamilton, Mary, 122
Hamilton, Sir William, 20, 26,
122 n., 171 n., 233
Hamilton, Mr., 231, 232
Hankey, Thomas, 202
Harcourt, George Simon, Earl,
62
Harding, Mr., 234
Hardwicke, *v.* Yorke
Harmsworth, Cecil, 58 n.
Hart, Emma, 20 n.
Hart, Mr., 11
Hastings, Warren, 76, 77 n.,
98, 234
Haverford College, 13 n.
Haward, Francis, 103 n., 245,
246, 248
Hely-Hutchinson, John, 215
Henkels, Stan V., 238
Henley, Robert, Earl of North-
ington, 175
Henry IV, 84 n.
Hervey, John Augustus, Earl,
212
Hill, Joseph, 166, 169
Hoare, Mr., 232
Hoare, Prince, 239
Hodges, William, 158, 192
Hogarth, William, 92
Homer, 218
Hone, Nathaniel, 25
Hood, Capt., 69, 231
Hood, Mrs., 231

266

Hoole, John, 79 n.
Hope, Henry, 86
Hope, John W., 86 n.
Horneck, Catherine and Mary, 54
Howard, Henry, 212
Hudson, Thomas, xix, 3, 4 n., 12, 189 n.
Hume, David, 39
Humphry, Mrs. George, 13, 240
Humphry, Ozias, 13, 14, 88, 227, 240
Hunter, William, 23, 238
Huntingdon, Henry E., 33 n., 239

Isaiah, 64, 65
Inchiquin, Earl of, 207 n.

James II, 101, 102
Jansen, Hendrik, 172, 205 n.
Jenkins, Thomas, 161, 174
Jervais, Thomas, 58–61, 95
Johnson, Elizabeth, 98
Johnson, Jane, 98
Johnson, Richard, 98, 233
Johnson, Samuel, letters to, 57, 75, 235; his spelling, xiv; on Vesey, 33 n.; reads *Zaphira* through, 41; on Banks, 67 n.; publishes Reynolds's essay on beauty, 93; attendance at the Club, 100; reads *The Village*, 101; *Dictionary* mentioned, 110 n., 140, 141, 219 n.; on Langton's children, 179 n.; and Mrs. Boswell's marmalade, 179 n.; connection with R.A., 181, 225; his monument, 123, 212, 215, 217, 222 n., 223, 236, 237, 251, 257 n., 258;

connection with Graves, 249, 250; mentioned, xi, xvi, xviii, xix, 40, 79 n., 140, 211, 223, 224, 257, 258
Johnson Society, 217 n., 250 n.
Johnson, William, xii, xxi, 76, 97, 205 n., 234, 236
Johnson, Mrs. William, 231
Jones, Polly, 29 n.
Jones, Sir William, 118 n.
Jordan, Mrs., 258
Joseph II, 81, 82, 129

Kageneck, Comte de, 129
Kauffman, Angelica, 37 n.
Kennedy, Matthew and Patrick, 29 n.
Kennedy, Polly, 29 n.
Keppel, Augustus, Lord, xiii, xix, 4 n., 5, 7, 68, 231
Kirby, Joshua, 15
Kirkley, Ralph, 217
Knight, Mr., 231, 237
Kraye, Lambert, 88

Lamb, Mr., 22
Lamb, W. R. M., xvii
Langton, Bennet, 67 n., 179, 181
Lawrence, Thomas, 214, 237
Leake, John M., 132
Leeds, *v.* Osborne
Leinster, Duchess of, 114
Lennox, Charles, third Duke of Richmond, 81
Lennox, Charles, fourth Duke of Richmond, 81
Lennox, Charlotte, 240
Leo X, 152
Leopold II, 48, 50, 203, 242, 243
Liddell, Anne, Countess of Upper Ossory, 71, 208, 209

Pembroke, Earl of, 159 n.
Pennsylvania Historical Society, 9 n., 110 n., 203 n.
Penny, Edward, 23
Percy, Thomas, 15, 31, 44, 100, 200, 234, 237, 252
Philidor, *v.* Danican
Philippe Égalité, 124
Philippo, 30
Pigot, Mrs., 231
Pindar, 149
Pine, Robert Edge, 11
Pine, Simon, 11
Pitt, John, Earl of Chatham, 111
Pitt, William, 132, 133, 138, 139 n.
Pliny, 28
Plutarch, 141
Pocock, Nicholas, 72
Poggi, Anthony, 47
Ponsonby, William, Earl of Bessborough, 161, 232
Pope, Alexander, xv, xvii, 62 n., 218, 250
Portland, Duke of, 151
Potemkin, Prince Gregory, 149
Pott, Mr., 236
Pott, Emily, 171 n.
Pottle, Frederick A., xvii
Poussin, Nicholas, 125, 126, 139, 145, 150, 160–165, 168, 175
Powell, L. F., 52 n.
Powels, Mr., 233
Pownall, Capt., 232
Price, F. N., 21 n.
Price, William, 11
Pringle, Sir John, 46, 67 n.
Prior, Matthew, 218
Public Advertiser, 44 n., 127 n.

Ramsay, Allan, xx, 112 n., 113

Raphael, 19, 87, 91, 162, 169, 218
Raton, Mr., 231
Rembrandt, 56 n., 242
Rennich, Mr., 233
Reynolds, Frances, 79, 239, 244
Reynolds, Frederic, 239
Reynolds, John, 3, 46
Reynolds, Sir Joshua, as letter-writer, xi–xvi; curriculum vitae, xix, xx; apprenticed to Hudson, 3; travels with Keppel, 4–8; studies in Italy, 9–13, 17, 19 n.; praises Humphry, 13, 14; employed by Newcastle, 14; calls on Percy, 15; declines directorship in Society of Artists, 15, 16; on establishment of R.A., 19, 22, 23; irritated by Hone, 25; thanks Hamilton for gift, 26; discusses pictures, 27, 29; admires Philippo, 30; elected Alderman of Plympton, 32; favours Vesey for Club, 33, 34; takes a holiday, 35; on ornamenting St. Paul's, 37, 38, 225; aids Joseph Palmer, 40–43, 110, 111, 150, 157, 162; on catalogue for Exhibition, 44, 45; recommends Waldré, 47; sends portrait to Florence, 48–51; encourages Northcote, 51, 52; wishes to oblige Mrs. Burke, 52, 53; comments on Indian drawings, 53; visits Blenheim, 54, 56; seeks help from Johnson, 57; plans West Window of New College Chapel, 58–61; entertains at dinner, 61, 70, 97, 126, 183, 184, 203, 227;

For EU product safety concerns, contact us at Calle de José Abascal, 56–1°, 28003 Madrid, Spain or eugpsr@cambridge.org.

 www.ingramcontent.com/pod-product-compliance
Ingram Content Group UK Ltd.
Pitfield, Milton Keynes, MK11 3LW, UK
UKHW012335130625
459647UK00009B/299

* 9 7 8 1 1 0 7 4 9 5 0 3 6 *